WORKBOOK

English Explorer 2

Jane Bailey
with Helen Stephenson

Australia • Brazil • Japan • Korea • Mexico • Singapore • Spain • United Kingdom • United States

English Explorer Workbook 2
Jane Bailey with Helen Stephenson

Publisher: Jason Mann

Adaptations Manager: Alistair Baxter

Assistant Editor: Manuela Barros

Product and Marketing Manager: Ruth McAleavey

Senior Content Project Editor: Natalie Griffith

Senior Production Controller: Paul Herbert

National Geographic Liaison: Leila Hishmeh

Cover Designer: Natasa Arsenidou

Text Designer: eMC Design Ltd., UK and PreMedia Global

Compositor: PreMedia Global

Audio: EFS Television Production Ltd.

Acknowledgments
The Publisher would like to thank the following for their invaluable contribution: Nick Sheard, Karen Spiller and Anna Cowper.

ISBN: 978-1-111-06268-2

National Geographic Learning
Cheriton House, North Way, Andover, Hampshire, SP10 5BE
United Kingdom

Cengage Learning is a leading provider of customized learning solutions with office locations around the globe, including Singapore, the United Kingdom, Australia, Mexico, Brazil and Japan. Locate your local office at: **international.cengage.com/region**

Cengage Learning products are represented in Canada by Nelson Education, Ltd.

Visit National Geographic Learning online at **ngl.cengage.com**

Visit our corporate website at **www.cengage.com**

Photo credits

The publishers would like to thank the following sources for permission to reproduce their copyright protected photographs:

Cover photo: Alaska Stock Images/National Geographic Image Collection

pp 4 (blaneyphoto/iStockphoto.com), 5 (vm/iStockphoto.com), 9 (BVDC – Fotolia.com), 10tl (Marion Wear – Fotolia.com), 10cl (kirza/iStockphoto.com), 10bl (Jupiterimages/Thinkstock/Alamy), 13 (aabejon/iStockphoto.com), 19 (mrva/iStockphoto.com), 22tr (shatteredlens/iStockphoto.com), 22tl (ftwitty/iStockphoto.com), 23a (emyerson/iStockphoto.com), 23b (pkruger/iStockphoto.com), 24 (Ira Block/National Geographic Image Collection), 30l (Clynt Garnham/Alamy), 30r (jpmediainc/iStockphoto.com), 32l (jhorrocks/iStockphoto.com), 32r (Gregory Wrona/Alamy), 33 (Charly – Fotolia.com), 34 (Image Source/Corbis), 35 (Vitaliy Pakhnyushchyy – Fotolia.com), 40 (Horace Bristol/Corbis), 41l (thornthunder/iStockphoto.com), 41r (larslentz/iStockphoto.com), 43 (Walt Disney/The Kobal Collection), 45tc (Ian West/PA Wire/Press Association Images), 45tr (Jim Smeal/BEI/Rex Features), 45br (Bettmann/Corbis), 53 (kentoh. Image from BigStockPhoto.com), 54 (Yui Mok/PA Archive/Press Association Images), 55a (Zakharchenko/iStockphoto.com), 55b (mountainberryphoto/iStockphoto.com), 55c (Orchidpoet – Fotolia.com), 55d (JoeGough/iStockphoto.com), 55bl (Galyna Andrushko – Fotolia.com), 56 (Rafa Irusta – Fotolia.com), 57 (Manxlad/iStockphoto.com), 58 (Ludwig Kriegl – Fotolia.com), 60 (Lee/iStockphoto.comDaniels), 64a (Alaska Stock LLC/Alamy), 64b (Razvan/iStockphoto.com), 64c (funkd/iStockphoto.com), 65 (George Steinmetz/National Geographic Image Collection), 67 (erwinova – Fotolia.com), 78a (monkeybusinessimages. Image from BigStockPhoto.com), 78b (JSABBOTT/iStockphoto.com), 78c (choja/iStockphoto.com), 78d (ktaylorg/iStockphoto.com), 85 (Oleander. Image from BigStockPhoto.com), 86 (Khrizmo/iStockphoto.com), 86 (Lee Karen Stow/Alamy), 86 (David Lyons/Alamy), 87 (slobo/iStockphoto.com), 89 (scanrail/iStockphoto.com), 90 (PaulCowan/iStockphoto.com), 96bg (Romko_chuk/iStockphoto.com), 96bl (ConstanceMcGuire/iStockphoto.com), 96br (Tatiana_Grozetskaya. Image from BigStockPhoto.com), 97bg (yegorius – Fotolia.com), 97tr (Steve and Donna O'Meara/National Geographic Image Collection), 97tc (_IuSh_/iStockphoto.com), 98t (Carsten Peter/National Geographic Image Collection), 98b (Bill Curtsinger/National Geographic Image Collection), 99t (Carsten Peter/National Geographic Image Collection), 100tr (Roy Toft/National Geographic Image Collection), 100cr (Will Mcintyre/Science Photo Library), 101bg (Muriel Lasure/Shutterstock, Inc), 101 (Herbert Kratky/Shutterstock, Inc), 101tr (topnat/iStockphoto.com), 102cr (Andrea Danti – Fotolia.com), 102bc (kati1313/iStockphoto.com), 102br (EML/Shutterstock, Inc), 103.1 (Paul Chesley/Stone/Getty Images), 103.2 (The Gallery Collection/Corbis), 103.3 (The Art Archive/Musée du Louvre Paris/Gianni Dagli Orti), 103.4 (Sandro Vannini/Corbis), 103.5 (Kirsten Soderlind/Corbis), 103bl (Juanmonino/iStockphoto.com), 104bg (Paul Sutherland/National Geographic Image Collection), 104tr (DavidOrr/iStockphoto.com), 104cl (Michael and Patricia Fogden/Minden Pictures/National Geographic Image Collection), 105tl (Chris Newbert/Minden Pictures/National Geographic Image Collection), 105tr (Snowleopard1/iStockphoto.com), 105cr (qldian. Image from BigStockPhoto.com), 105b (Ameng Wu/123rf.com), 106 (Fred Mayer/Hulton Archive/Getty Images), 107bg (James L. Stanfield/National Geographic Image Collection), 107tl (Natalia Pavlova – Fotolia.com), 107cl (YinYang/iStockphoto.com), 108 (Robb Kendrick/National Geographic Image Collection), 109bg (Royal Geographical Society 2005/Edmund Hillary), 109 (Tad Welch/National Geographic Image Collection), 109 (Tad Welch/National Geographic Image Collection), 110 (Zuki/iStockphoto.com), 111 (Galyna Andrushko – Fotolia.com)

Illustrations by Nigel Dobbyn pp 3tr, 8, 18tl, 24cr/br, 29, 42tl/br, 56l, 74b, 88, 109; Celia Hart pp 3b, 18tr, 22, 40, 43, 63, 73cl, 74t, 94; Tim Kahane pp 11, 13; Martin Sanders pp 18b, 54, 57, 87, 100, 111; Eric Smith pp 5, 19, 20, 21, 24tr, 31, 42tr, 51, 62r, 73bl, 76; Simon Tegg p 30; Mark Turner pp 34, 62l, 68

Printed in the United Kingdom by Ashford Colour Press Ltd.
Print Number: 09 Print Year: 2024

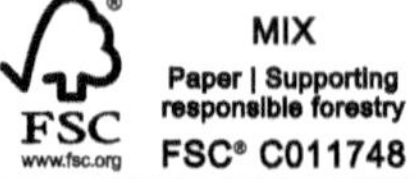

At school

Vocabulary: classroom objects

1 Complete the description of the classroom.

This is a picture of our classroom. It's a big room and there's a large [1]................................ at the front of the class. There are a lot of [2]................................ and chairs. On the wall near the door, there's a [3]................................ and a big [4]................................ for the week. We've also got a [5]................................ .... so we can do listening exercises. We can see the sports field from a big [6]................................ at the back of the class.

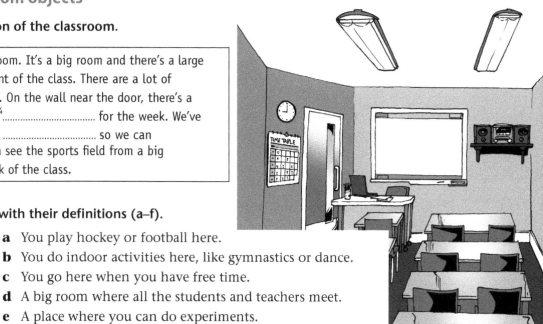

2 Match the words (1–6) with their definitions (a–f).

1 playground
2 sports field
3 science laboratory
4 dining room
5 hall
6 gym

a You play hockey or football here.
b You do indoor activities here, like gymnastics or dance.
c You go here when you have free time.
d A big room where all the students and teachers meet.
e A place where you can do experiments.
f You eat here.

Grammar: *have got* (affirmative and negative)

3 Complete the table.

	Long form	Short form	Short answers	
I	....	I've got	Yes, I	No, I ....
You	have got	....	Yes, you have.	No, you haven't.
He	has got	....	Yes, ...	No, ...
She	....	....	....	....
It	....	....	....	....
We	have got	....	....	....
They	....	....	....	....

4 Look at the pictures and write sentences. Say what the people in the classroom *have* or *haven't got*. Use short forms.

Mr Benson *Mr Benson's got a dictionary and a notebook but he hasn't got a pencil.*

2 Sally ....

1 Linda ....

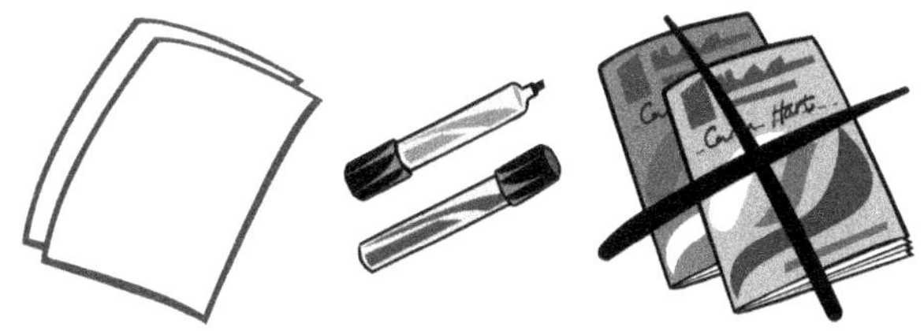

3 Karim and Neil ....

Grammar: *have got* (question forms and short answers)

5 Write the questions and give short answers.

your school / a playground?

Has your school got a playground? Yes, it has.

1 you / an English dictionary?

....

2 your teacher / a red pen?

....

3 your classroom / a clock?

....

4 you and your classmates / workbooks?

....

5 your school / a sports field?

....

6 the teachers / a dining room?

....

Vocabulary: school subjects

6 Read the clues and complete the crossword.

ACROSS

2 You paint and draw.
4 Tu parles français.
6 You study plants and the human body.
8 You learn about the past.
10 You do experiments in a laboratory.
12 You use a computer.

DOWN

1 You learn about numbers and how they work.
3 You use this book.
5 You study how things work.
7 You learn about countries.
9 You do sport.
11 You sing and play instruments.

Reading and listening

7 S1 Read and listen to Emily. Complete the timetable.

Hi. I'm Emily and I'm in Class 2, Year 9 at Longtown High School. This term our timetable's OK. On Monday and Wednesday we've got art and music in the morning. After the break, we've got maths and biology. In the afternoon, we've got double English. On Tuesday, we do a lot of science. In the morning, we've got chemistry and physics, then we've got history and biology after the break. In the afternoon, we've got French and PE. On Thursday, we've got history and geography in the morning and maths and chemistry after the break. In the afternoon, we've got French and IT. On Friday, we've got double geography in the morning, then chemistry and IT after the break. In the afternoon we've got music and art. I love music and art, so we've got a great start to the week and a fantastic end to the week, too.

	Mon	Tues	Wed	Thurs	Fri
9.00	art	chemistry	art	5	geography
9.50	music	2	music	geography	7 ....
10.40	break				
11.00	1	history	maths	maths	chemistry
11.50	biology	biology	biology	6	IT
12.40	lunch				
1.55	English	French	4	French	8 ....
14.45	English	3	English	IT	music

8 Answer the questions about the timetable. Write full sentences.

When has Emily got double English?

She's got double English on Monday and Wednesday afternoon.

1 When has Emily got PE?

She ....

2 Which days has she got music?

....

3 What time is morning break?

It ....

4 What time is lunch?

....

5 Have Class 2 got history on Thursday morning?

....

6 Have they got science on Friday afternoon?

....

STARTER

In class

Useful expressions

1 Match the expressions (1–5) with the responses (a–e).

1 Can I borrow your rubber? *b*
2 Can you help me?
3 What does 'busy' mean?
4 How do you spell 'expression'?
5 Can I go to the toilet, please?

a No, I'm sorry. I'm busy at the moment.
b Yes, of course. Here you are.
c Can you wait until the break? It's only two minutes!
d I don't know. Ask the teacher.
e I think it means 'happy'.

2 Look at the situations. Write the expressions. Use the words in brackets.

(toilet) *Can I go to the toilet, please?*

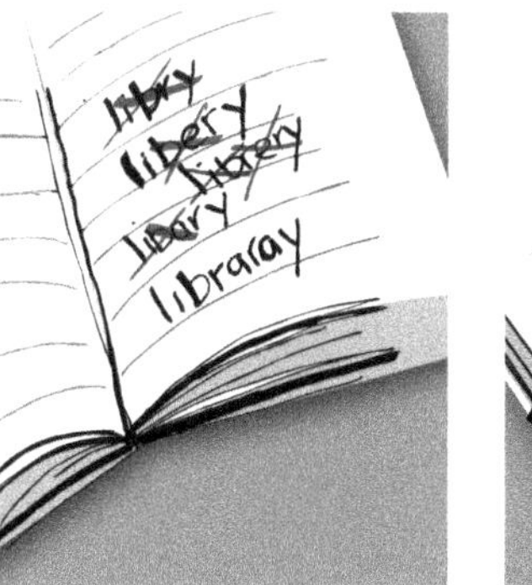

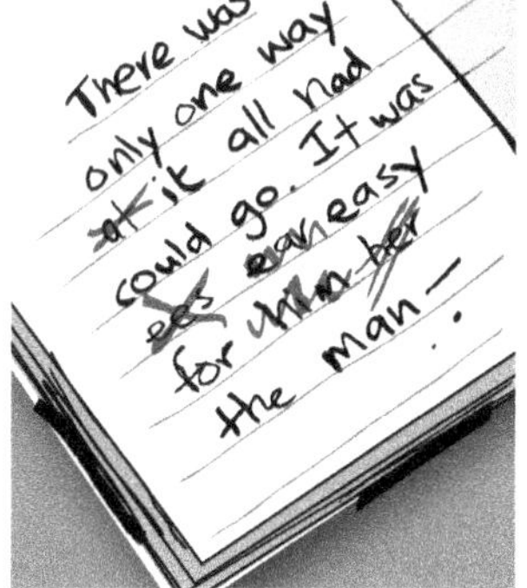

1 (spell) ....
....
..............................?

3 (borrow) ....
....
..............................?

2 (mean) ....
....
..............................?

4 (help) ....
....
..............................?

Grammar: *there is / there are*

3 Read about *English Explorer* Workbook 2. Are the sentences true or false?

	T	F
There is a Review after every two units.	✔	☐
1 There are eight units.	☐	☐
2 There are two pages of *Grammar Practice* exercises after each unit.	☐	☐
3 There aren't any colour photographs.	☐	☐
4 There is a reading text in each unit.	☐	☐
5 There are word lists for each unit.	☐	☐

4 a Complete the grammar box for *there is / there are*.

Singular noun		Plural noun	
+	–	+	–
there is	....	....	....

b Write sentences about your classroom. Use the words in the box.

~~window~~ board chairs clock timetable CD player desks

In my classroom there are four windows.

1 ....
2 ....
3 ....
4 ....
5 ....
6 ....

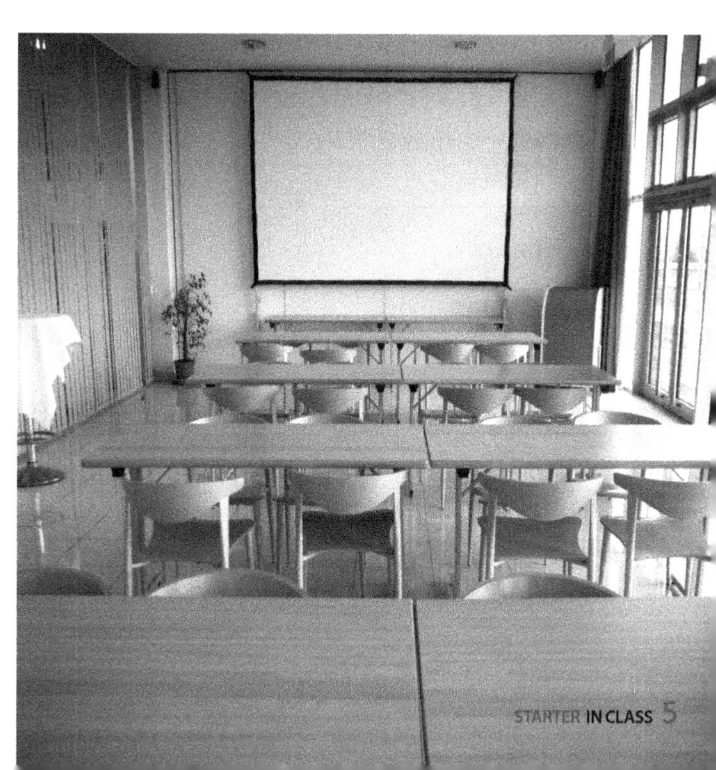

Grammar: *can*

5 Look at the table. Write about Sally and Karim.

Can you	Sally	Karim	You
1 count to 100 in French?	Yes	No	
2 cook a meal?	No	Yes	
3 name three school subjects in French?	Yes	No	
4 drive a car?	No	No	
5 sing a song in English?	Yes	Yes	
6 ride a bike?	Yes	Yes	
7 use a dictionary?	No	Yes	

Sally

count / to 100 / in French

Sally can count to 100 in French.

1 name / three school subjects / in French
She ....

2 cook / a meal
She ....

Karim

1 cook / a meal
Karim ....

2 use / a dictionary
He ....

3 name / three school subjects / in French
He ....

Karim and Sally

1 ride / a bike
Karim and Sally ....

2 sing a song / in English
They ....

3 drive / a car
They ....

6 Now complete the table in Exercise 5 about you. Then write two sentences with *can* and two sentences with *can't*.

I can count to 100 in French.

can
1 2
can't
3 4

7 Write questions and short answers with *can*.

Karim / cook a meal

Can Karim cook a meal? Yes, he can.

1 Sally / name three school subjects in French?
....

2 Karim / use a dictionary?
....

3 you / sing a song in English?
....

4 Sally and Karim / ride a bike?
....

5 Sally and Karim / drive a car?
....

6 you / cook a meal?
....

Working with words: nouns and verbs

8 Complete the table.

Noun	Verb
....	help
expression	express
....	mean
practice	....
....	spell
....	translate
writing / writer	....

9 Use the words in the table in Exercise 8 to complete the sentences.

'Can I go to the toilet, please?' is a useful *expression*.

1 Can you .... me, please?

2 You can find the .... of words in a dictionary.

3 What does 'each' .... ?

4 There is a .... of the words in each unit in the word list.

5 English .... can be difficult.

6 There is a .... exercise in each unit of this book.

STARTER

Friends and family

1 a Look at the picture and read the description. Write the names of Sally's friends.

1 *Sally* **2** .... **3** .... **4** ....

Sally is in the park with her friends. Sally has got [1] .... hair and Leticia has got very dark hair. Sally is tall and she's wearing [2] ...., a grey top and [3] .... Leticia isn't very tall. She's wearing a [4] .... and a white [5] ....
Darren and Karim have got brown hair. Darren is very tall and [6] .... He's wearing school trousers and a [7] .... Karim is wearing jeans and a [8] ....

b Complete the descriptions. Use the words in the box.

slim	fair	sweatshirt	jacket	skirt
jeans	trainers	shirt		

2 Look at the picture in Exercise 1. Write the names.

He's got a school bag. *Darren*
1 She's wearing earrings. ....
2 He's got a sports bag. ....
3 She's got a drink. ....
4 She's happy. ....
5 He's got a watch. ....

Listening

3 S.2 Listen to the interview with Sasha talking about her family. Tick the countries you hear.

Italy	Wales	Austria	Scotland
Germany	Spain	Poland	

4 Listen again. Are the sentences true or false?

	T	F
1 Sasha's got three children.	☐	☐
2 Her son's got two sons.	☐	☐
3 Sasha's got three grandchildren.	☐	☐
4 Her favourite cousin lives in Poland.	☐	☐
5 Gosia's favourite food is pasta.	☐	☐

Grammar: 's

5 Write *is* or *has* or possessive.

Gosia's favourite food is pasta. *possessive*
1 My bag's brown. ....
2 Stephanie's got two children. ....
3 Albert's thirty. ....
4 There's a pen on the desk. ....
5 What's Karim got? ....
6 My sister's name is Ann. ....

6 Look at the form. Write the question for each line of information.

Longtown Sports Club
1 Anna
2 Smith
3 21 Green Lane, Longtown LO9 7YG
4 01154 487631
5 15
6 swimming, badminton, running
7 18th, August 1995

1 *What's your name?*
2 ....
3 ....
4 ....
5 ....
6 ....
7 ....

1A Student profiles

Vocabulary: likes and dislikes

1 a Match the words from column A with the words from column B.

A	B
read	the housework
do	TV
watch	computer games
do	books
tidy	homework
play	their bedroom

b Look at the pictures and write sentences. Use the *-ing* form of the verb.

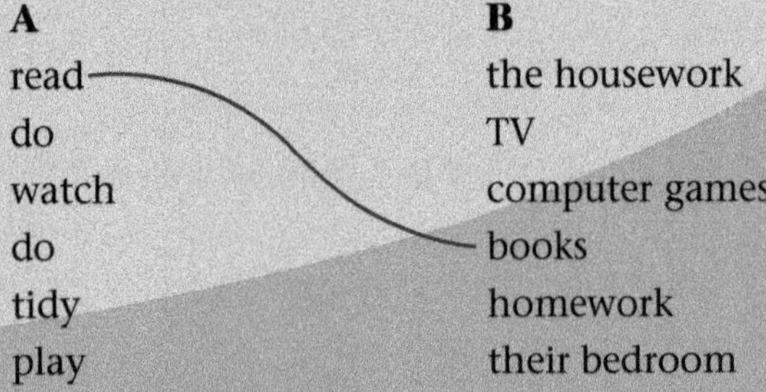

1 Alison loves ....

2 The boys like ....

3 Patrick doesn't like ....

4 Theo hates ....

5 Judith likes ....

6 The girls don't like ....

Grammar: present simple

2 Complete the sentences with the present simple form of the verbs in brackets.

Mia and Kate *go* to the same high school. (go)

1 They .... in the second year. (be)

2 I .... my mother with the housework. (help)

3 We .... art and music. (love)

4 Penny .... sport and maths. (not like)

5 Mia .... computer games after school. (play)

6 My brother .... a lot of books. (read)

Grammar: present simple questions

3 Complete the interview. Write the questions and short answers.

Hello Sandra. you / go / high school? (✔)

Hello Sandra. Do you go to high school?
Yes, I do.

1 you / like your school? (✔)

....

2 your brother / do his homework every night? (✘)

....

3 you and your friends / meet after school? (✔)

....

4 your sister / help with the housework? (✘)

....

5 your parents / watch TV in the evening? (✘)

....

6 they / play computer games? (✔)

....

7 I / ask good questions? (✘)

....

4 Eve is asking Ruby about her spare time activities. Complete the dialogue with the words in the box.

do (x3)	does	doesn't	go	play	sing

Eve: Do you ....*do*.......... any sports, Ruby?

Ruby: Yes, I 1 .... I 2 .... tennis and hockey.

Eve: Me too! I love tennis.

Ruby: Yeah. It's great, isn't it? But hockey's fantastic! I'm in the school team.

Eve: Wow! You're very sporty. 3 .... you have any other interests?

Ruby: Yes. I 4 .... to dance classes. And me and my friend 5 .... in a band. I'm the lead singer and she's the drummer.

Eve: Really?! What's the name of your band?

Ruby: Well. We're all girls, so we're called *Girl Power*.

Eve: That's a good name.

Ruby: Thanks.

Eve: 6 .... your friend dance, too?

Ruby: No, she 7 .... She's a terrible dancer!

Working with words: *-ing* forms

5 Complete the sentences with the *-ing* form of the verbs in brackets.

I love *doing* sports. (do)

1 I like .... to music. (listen)

2 My parents don't like .... computer games. (play)

3 My dog loves .... in the river. (swim)

4 Our cat hates .... a bath. (have)

5 I love .... emails to my friends. (write)

6 Do you like .... your bedroom? (tidy)

6 Write sentences and questions.

I / love / play / basketball *I love playing basketball.*

1 My brother / hate / sing

....

2 We / like / watch TV

....

3 Our mum / not like / cycle

....

4 My friends / not like / help with the housework

....

5 you / like / go to concerts?

....

6 Jack / like / cook?

....

7 Complete the paragraph about Jack. Write the present simple or the *-ing* form of the verbs in the box.

be	cook	do	help (x2)	play

Jack is 14. He goes to Redhill High School in Lancaster, in the north of England. His favourite subjects 1 .... science and sports. After school, he 2 .... his homework and 3 .... tennis. At the weekend, he 4 .... his mother. He hates 5 .... with the housework, but he likes 6 ....

1B Performers

Reading

1 **Look at the photos of three young musicians. Match them with the names and instruments.**

Gareth McBride: percussion Mark Fontainebleau: trumpet Sammy Li: violin

1 ....

2 ....

3 ....

2 **Read about Mark Fontainebleau. Choose the best heading (a–d) for each paragraph (1–3). There is one extra heading.**

a Activities and interests	c School and studies
b Favourite instruments	d Music and family

Young Musician of the Year

1 ....

Mark Fontainebleau plays the trumpet and is a finalist in the *Young Musician of the Year* competition. He is eighteen years old and is a student at Sunningdale High School in Wycombe, England, where he studies music, physics and maths. Every week he travels to the Guildhall School of Music and Drama in London.

2 ....

Mark plays in a symphony orchestra and in a jazz quartet with three friends. He always practises hard. When he is in a competition, he sometimes practises for six hours a day. He doesn't come from a musical family. He's got a brother who likes trying different instruments but he never plays anything for very long. His parents don't play an instrument.

3 ....

In his free time, Mark likes doing puzzles and playing chess. He loves jazz music, of course, and often listens to other famous jazz trumpeters. He doesn't usually listen to modern pop music. Mark also likes watching films and eating good food. He likes spending time with his friends and with his girlfriend. And he loves sleeping.

3 **Read the text again. Are the sentences true or false?**

	T	F
Mark goes to school in Wycombe.	☑	☐
1 He studies music and drama at school.	☐	☐
2 He travels to music school in London every day.	☐	☐
3 He always practises for six hours every day.	☐	☐
4 He often plays in a quartet with his brother.	☐	☐
5 He doesn't like listening to pop music.	☐	☐

Listening

4 **1.1 Listen to an interview with another finalist from the *Young Musician of the Year* competition. Answer the questions.**

1 Look at the photos in Exercise 1 on page 10. Which young musician is it?

2 Look at the pictures. Put a tick (✔) next to the instruments they play.

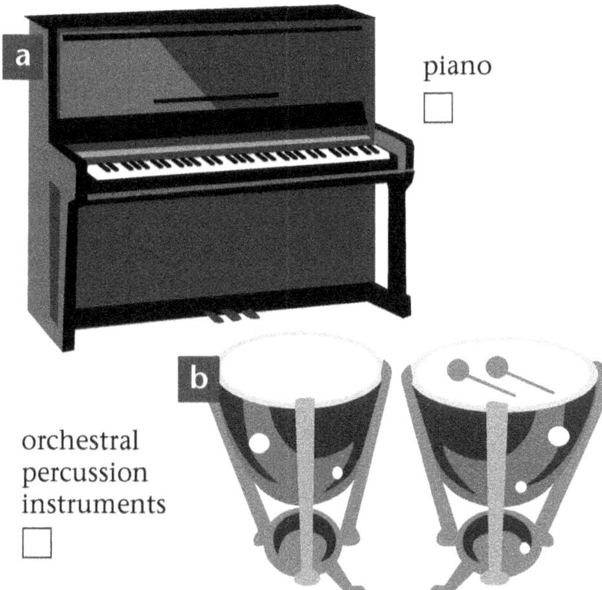

5 **Listen again and circle the correct option.**

Sammy plays *the violin / the piano.*

1 She plays in *an orchestra / a jazz band* at school.

2 She performs with a folk band *at festivals / at school.*

3 She's also in *a rock group / an orchestra* called *The Electric Symphony.*

4 In her free time, she *usually / sometimes* plays badminton.

5 She *likes / doesn't like* watching other bands perform.

Vocabulary: performing

6 **Circle the odd word out.**

Actors *take part in / act / do* in films.

1 Clowns wear a *costume / make-up / an instrument.*

2 Do you *act / sing / play* in a band?

3 We take part in a *show / a costume / a festival* every summer.

4 The Smith family perform in *an instrument / a circus / a show* every weekend.

5 Can you do *magic / a costume / your own make-up?*

6 What instrument do you *act / like best / play?*

Grammar: adverbs of frequency

7 **Choose the correct adverb and put it in the correct position in the sentence.**

Mark practises for six hours every day. (sometimes / always)

Mark sometimes practises for six hours every day.

1 Circus clowns wear a costume. (sometimes / always)

2 Our band takes part in festivals in the summer. It's great fun! (never / often)

3 Madonna dances when she sings. (usually / never)

4 Johnny Depp acts in adventure films. (never / sometimes)

5 My favourite band only performs in the big cities. They perform in my town. (never / sometimes)

6 The people in the audience at a pop concert sing. (never / often)

7 I don't like watching plays so I don't go to the theatre. (often / sometimes)

8 My family loves watching films. We watch a DVD at the weekends. (always / never)

1C Making suggestions

Useful expressions: making suggestions

1 Tom is talking to his dad about making new friends. Complete the dialogue with suggestions from the box.

Aha! How about photography? There's a club on Tuesdays. What about joining the school choir? ~~I know. How about doing some after-school activities?~~ Why don't you do some ballet classes? Well, let's look at the list, then.

AFTER-SCHOOL CLUBS

Monday	–	choir
Tuesday	–	photography
Wednesday	–	ballet
Thursday	–	sports club
Friday	–	chess

Tom: It's difficult to make friends at my new school.

Dad: *I know. How about doing some after-school activities?*

Tom: Great idea! But, what? I don't like sports.

Dad: 1 ....

Tom: What? I can't dance and I can't even touch my toes!

Dad: Yes. But it's brilliant exercise. And there are a lot of girls there!

Tom: Dad!

Dad: OK. Let's think about this seriously. What's that paper you've got in your hand?

Tom: It's a list of clubs.

Dad: 2 ....

Tom: OK. Here you are.

Dad: Hmm. 3 ....

Tom: I don't like singing.

Dad: 4 ....

Tom: Yeah. Good idea. I can learn how to use Photoshop.

2 Tom is talking to his new friends, Andrea and Justin. Complete the dialogue with the correct form of the verbs in brackets.

Andrea: How about 1 .... (go) to the arts festival this year?

Justin: Great idea! It's usually really good. What's on this year?

Andrea: Well, there's a lot of music, and theatre and street performances.

Tom: Sounds brilliant! I love live music. What about 2 .... (go) to see some bands perform?

Justin: Yes. We can do that on Saturday. Let's 3 .... (see) some theatre groups, too.

Andrea: Good idea. We can do that on Sunday. Why don't we 4 .... (buy) the tickets today? The festival's very popular and the tickets sell fast.

Tom: I agree. But let's 5 .... (decide) exactly what we want to do first. And what about 6 .... (take) a tent and camping overnight?

Justin: Yeah. Great idea, Tom.

Andrea: Right, then. Let's 7 .... (look) at the programme.

Pronunciation: syllables

3 a 1.2 Listen to these words and write them in the correct column.

drum concert musician play orchestra school cooking festival choir friend grandparents vegetables instrument programme music

one syllable	two syllables	three syllables
....	....	....
....	....	....
....	....	....
....	....	....
....	....	....
....	....	....

Vocabulary: musical instruments

4 Find the names of 10 musical instruments in the word square.

S	Y	N	T	H	E	S	I	Z	E	R
A	F	C	D	G	K	D	R	U	M	S
X	Y	L	O	P	H	O	N	E	B	K
O	H	A	R	P	N	U	W	X	I	P
P	P	R	M	I	L	S	J	F	E	I
H	V	I	O	L	I	N	H	L	U	A
O	O	N	U	K	W	S	Y	U	A	N
N	L	E	A	Z	S	C	W	T	H	O
E	Z	T	T	R	U	M	P	E	T	C

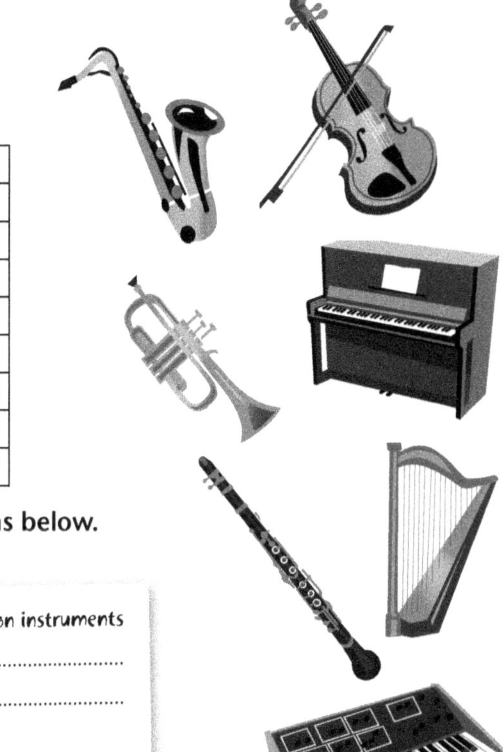

5 Write the names of the instruments from Exercise 4 in the columns below. Can you add more instruments to each column?

String instruments	Wind instruments	Keyboard	Percussion instruments
......violin......	....	....	....
....	....	....	....
	....		
	....		

Writing: a personal profile

6 Read Leila's profile and fill in the gaps. Use information from the notes below.

Profile

Hi. I'm Leila and I'm [1] .... I go to [2] .... School. My favourite subjects are [3] ...., art, physics and [4] .... In my free time, I love doing [5] .... and I sometimes perform at children's parties. My ambition is to be a [6] .... I also like [7] .... and [8] .... chess with my Dad. I usually lose! What are my weak points? Well, I don't always do my homework. My good points are I often help my mum with the [9] .... and I always [10] .... hard for exams.
Do you like my profile? Why don't you click on my photo and write to me?

1 age: 14
2 school: Castle High School
3 favourite subjects: English, art, physics, chemistry
4 free-time interests: magic, performing magic at parties, swimming, playing chess
5 ambition: to be a famous magician
6 weak points: don't always do my homework
7 good points: help my mum with the housework, study for exams

7 Complete the notes with Tom's interests. Then write Tom's profile. Look at Leila's profile in Exercise 6 for help.

1 age: 14
2 school: Redhill High School, Lancaster
3 favourite subjects: physics, art, maths
4 after-school interests: drawing, m.................................... and p....................................
5 ambition: to be a famous photographer
6 weak points: don't do sports, don't tidy my room
7 good points: study for exams, play with my little sister

Study tip!

Remember to join sentences with 'and'.

1D Explore more

Reading

1 Read the text on the right. Decide which sentences (1–4) below are true and which are false.

	T	F
La Tomatina is a festival in Spain.	✔	☐
1 La Tomatina lasts one week.	☐	☐
2 There is a tomato fight every day.	☐	☐
3 There is music and dancing during the festival.	☐	☐
4 Only people from Buñol take part in the tomato fight.	☐	☐

La Tomatina is a famous festival in Spain. It takes place during the last week of August in a town called Buñol, in Valencia.

During the festival there is music, parades, dancing and fireworks. The last day of the festival is always a Wednesday. On this day, there is an enormous tomato fight. People come from all over the world to take part and more than one hundred tons of very ripe tomatoes are thrown in the streets. The tomato fight can be very brutal. It is a tradition for the women to wear white and the men to wear no shirts.

The night before the tomato fight there is a paella cooking competition.

2 Read the text again and complete the sentences with one word.

1. During the festival, people .... tomatoes at each other.
2. The paella cooking competition is on .... night.

3 Read the text. Decide which sentences (1–4) are true and which are false. Then complete the sentences (5–6) with one word in each gap.

The Edinburgh Festival takes place in August every year in Edinburgh, Scotland. It is the biggest arts festival in the world. There isn't just one festival but lots of festivals which take place at the same time.

The main festival is called the Edinburgh International Festival. Famous actors and performers come from all over the world to take part in classical theatre, opera, music and dance.

The Edinburgh Fringe Festival is also very famous. It includes alternative theatre and comedy as well as children's shows and musicals. A lot of the performers are students from university or people from small theatre groups. There are also many street performances.

1. The Edinburgh Festival takes place in Scotland.
2. There are lots of different festivals in Edinburgh in August.
3. The Edinburgh International Festival is a pop music festival.
4. You can see classical opera at the Fringe Festival.
5. Many performers at the Fringe Festival are university ....
6. At the Fringe Festival some people perform in the ....

Listening

4 Look at the notes below. What type of information is missing in each gap? Complete the gaps (1–6) with the information (a–f).

Saturday Club

Where? Longtown [1] ......c......

When? Saturday afternoons, from [2] .... p.m. to 6 p.m.

What? Different activities – sports, e.g. [3] .... basketball, badminton and tennis and other activities – team games, jazz dance and [4] ....

Who? Teenagers aged twelve to [5] ....

Telephone: 01530 [6] ....

a name of a sport
b age
c ~~name of a place~~
d time
e telephone number
f name of an activity

5 1.3 Listen to a radio advertisement for a sports club and complete the notes in Exercise 4 with the correct information.

6 1.4 Listen to a conversation about the Saturday Club and complete the sentences.

Frank usually [1] .... or reads [2] .... on Saturday afternoons.
He likes [3] .... but he doesn't like [4] .... He loves [5] ....
Deepak telephones the [6] ....

7 1.5 Listen to an interview with a teacher at Longtown Sports Centre. Complete the notes.

Name:	[1] ....
Classes she teaches:	[2] ...., jazz dance and hip hop.
Number of pupils doing ballet:	[3] .... boys and 46 girls.
Age of students:	[4] .... to sixteen.
Interests:	Dancing and singing – performs in [5] ...., theatre, and [6] ....

Word list Starter Unit and Unit 1

adventure (adj) ....
audience (n) ....
blow (v) ....
bite (v) ....
brass instrument (n) ....
capital (n) ....
caption (n) ....
carnival (n) ....
chess (n) ....
choir (n) ....
circle (n) ....
clap (v) ....
clarinet (n) ....
classmate (n) ....
collide (v) ....
competition (n) ....
construction (n) ....
crazy (adj) ....
curtain (n) ....
cycle (v) ....
day-to-day (phr) ....
different (adj) ....
double (adj) ....
earring (n) ....
Earth's atmosphere (phr) ....
electric particles (phr) ....
express (v) ....
expression (n) ....
flash (n) ....
fight (v) ....
flute (n) ....
folk (adj) ....
forest (n) ....
gas (n) ....
generation (n) ....
good points (phr) ....
harp (n) ....
homework (n) ....
housework (n) ....
hungry (adj) ....
hunt (v) ....
indoor (n) ....
interest (n) ....
interview (n) ....
join (v) ....
judge (n) ....
lead (adj) ....
look after (phr v) ....
lose (v) ....
magnetic fields (phr) ....
make up (n) ....
moist air (phr) ....
occasion (n) ....
overnight (adv) ....
pasta (n) ....
pattern (n) ....
percussion (n) ....
perform (v) ....
performance (n) ....
performer (n) ....
playground (n) ....
practise (v) ....
preparation (n) ....
prism (n) ....
raindrops (n) ....
rare (adj) ....
ripe (adj) ....
river (n) ....
shape (n) ....
skateboarding (n) ....
spectacular (adj) ....
spend (v) ....
split (v) ....
sporty (adj) ....
stick (n) ....
string (n) ....
subject (n) ....
sunset (n) ....
synthesiser (n) ....
take part (phr v) ....
take photographs (phr) ....
terrible (adj) ....
ticket (n) ....
tribal (adj) ....
trumpet (n) ....
vegetable (n) ....
violin (n) ....
weak (adj) ....
weak points (phr) ....
wear (v) ....
wind instrument (n) ....
winner (n) ....
wooden (adj) ....
woodwind instrument (n) ....

U1 Reading Explorer

bite (v) ....
collide (v) ....
curtain (n) ....
Earth's atmosphere (phr) ....
electric particles (phr) ....
flash (n) ....
gas (n) ....
magnetic fields (phr) ....
moist air (phr) ....
prism (n) ....
raindrops (n) ....
rare (adj) ....
shape (n) ....
split (v) ....
sunset (n) ....

Grammar Practice Unit 1

present simple

We use **present simple** to talk about things that are always true, things we do often or that happen often, etc.

*The sun **rises** in the east.*

*My grandmother **lives** in Trinidad.*

*I **watch** TV every evening.*

In the affirmative, we add **-s** to the verb after *he*, *she* or *it*.

I/You/We/They enjoy dancing.

He/She/It enjoys reading.

> With verbs ending in ***-ss***, ***-sh***, ***-ch***, ***-x*** and ***-o***, we add ***-es***.
>
> passes washes watches fixes does
>
> With verbs ending in a **consonant** + ***-y***, we change the ***-y*** to ***-ies***.
>
> study studies worry worries

In the negative, we use ***don't*** or ***doesn't*** and the bare infinitive of the main verb. We DON'T add ***–s*** or ***–es*** to the main verb.

*I **don't** like doing homework.*

*My little brother **doesn't** go to school.*

Affirmative		
I/You/We/They	love	carnivals.
He/She/It	loves	
Negative		
I/You/We/They	don't (do not)	play computer games.
He/She/It	doesn't (does not)	

1 Complete the sentences with the present simple form of the verbs in brackets.

We *go* to the same school. (**go**)

1 Carol .... the trumpet in the school orchestra. (**play**)
2 I usually .... my friends after school. (**meet**)
3 Kate .... acting. (**love**)
4 My mum .... great cakes. (**make**)
5 Fekria .... her mother with the housework. (**help**)
6 We .... the Internet at school. (**use**)
7 Miriam .... really well. (**dance**)
8 You and your sister .... a lot of books! (**read**)

2 Complete the sentences with the present simple form of the verbs in brackets.

Fekria *studies* very hard. (**study**)

1 Fekria always .... the dishes to help her mother. (**wash**)
2 She also .... her bedroom. (**tidy**)
3 Jamie .... his homework after school. (**do**)
4 He .... TV every night. (**watch**)
5 He also .... skateboarding in his free time. (**go**)

3 Complete the sentences with *don't* or *doesn't*.

Will *doesn't* think about school in the evening.

1 My sister and I .... go to the same school.
2 Judy .... play a musical instrument.
3 Jamie .... want to be a doctor.
4 Judy and Kate .... speak Italian.
5 I .... like tidying my bedroom.
6 My parents .... play computer games.
7 Terry .... walk to school – he cycles.
8 You .... know my friend Sara.

4 Write sentences in the present simple with these words. Use short forms.

Fiona / sing / beautifully / but she / not play / the piano

Fiona sings beautifully but she doesn't play the piano.

1 I / study Spanish / but I / not speak / it very well

....

2 He / like / reading / but he / not study / hard

....

3 They / live / in the UK / but they / not live / in London

....

4 Angela / read / lots of books / but she / not read / comics

....

5 Ricky / do / some housework / but he / not wash / the dishes

....

We make questions by putting ***do*** or ***does*** before the subject, and then the bare infinitive of the main verb. We DON'T add ***–s*** or ***–es*** to the main verb.

***Do** you **like** skateboarding?*

***Does** he **go** to your school?*

In short answers, we don't use the main verb.

*Does your grandmother live in Trinidad? – Yes, she **does**.*

*Do they play in the orchestra? – No, they **don't**.*

Questions			
Do	I/you/we/they	play computer games?	
Does	he/she/it		
Short answers			
Yes, I/you/we/they	do.	No, I/you/we/they	don't.
Yes, he/she/it	does.	No, he/she/it	doesn't.

5 Complete the questions with *Do* or *Does*.

Do you like acting?

1 .... Fekria want to be a doctor?
2 .... we study the same subjects?
3 .... I sing well?
4 .... Adam and Lewis play in the orchestra?
5 .... you send your friends text messages?
6 .... your mum and dad speak English?
7 .... Will play the drums?

6 Write questions from these sentences.

The theatre group meets every Wednesday.
Does the theatre group meet every Wednesday?

1 They organise a carnival every year.
....
2 Everyone joins in the carnival.
....
3 People dance in the streets.
....
4 Steel bands play calypso music.
....
5 Calypso music comes from Trinidad.
....
6 The police enjoy the carnival too.
....

7 Put the words into the correct order to make questions.

meet / the theatre group / does / at four o'clock?
Does the theatre group meet at four o'clock?

1 do / live / Adam and Lewis / in Australia?
....
2 Kate / love / does / acting?
....
3 need / do / we / singing lessons?
....
4 to be / Fekria / want / does / a musician?
....
5 do / does / his homework / Jamie / after school?
....

8 Now write affirmative (✔) or negative (✘) short answers to the questions in Exercise 7.

(Does the theatre group meet at four o'clock?) (✔)
Yes, it does.

1 (✘) ....
2 (✔) ....
3 (✔) ....
4 (✘) ....
5 (✔) ....

Adverbs of frequency

We use adverbs of frequency to talk about habits or how often something happens.

100% ←————————→ 0%

always usually often sometimes never

Adverbs of frequency go before the main verb.
She ***often*** *practises the piano.*
They don't ***always*** *help their mum with the housework.*
BUT they go after the verb ***be***.
It is ***usually*** *warm in the summer.*
We are ***never*** *late for school.*

9 Put the adverbs in the correct place.

The theatre group meets in room seven. **(always)**
The theatre group always meets in room seven.

1 Rob isn't at home on Saturdays. **(often)**
....
2 I forget my best friend's birthday. **(never)**
....
3 The carnival is lots of fun. **(always)**
....
4 Will practises the drums in the evening. **(usually)**
....
5 My parents help me with my homework. **(sometimes)**
....

10 Put the words into the correct order to make sentences.

spectacular / always / are / the carnival costumes
The carnival costumes are always spectacular.

1 listen to / sometimes / classical music / I
....
2 meet / my friends and I / usually / after school
....
3 are / there / lots of people / always / at the school concert
....
4 never / for her violin lesson / is / Charlotte / late
....
5 we / eat / for dinner / pizza / often
....

2A Hurricane hunters

Vocabulary: jobs

1 Write the job under each picture.

a factory worker

1 a .... 2 a .... 3 a ....

4 a .... 5 a .... 6 a ....

2 Match the definitions (1–6) with the jobs (a–f).

1 I tell people about the news. You can sometimes see me on TV.
2 I work in a restaurant or a bar. I take food and drink to customers.
3 People bring their animals to me when they are ill. I sometimes do operations.
4 I invent stories. My books are famous all over the world.
5 I work in a laboratory and do experiments.
6 I take things from the factory to supermarkets and shops.

a writer
b reporter
c truck driver
d scientist
e vet
f waiter

3 Complete the lists.

1 People who work in a hospital: *dentist*, do.........................., nu..........................
2 People who usually work outside: fa.........................., bu..........................
3 People who work in an office: of.........................., re..........................
4 People with jobs that can be dangerous: fi.........................., po..........................
5 People who usually wear a uniform at work: po.........................., pi.........................., nu.........................., fi..........................

Vocabulary: weather

4 Match the words (1–8) with the pictures (a–h).

1 cloudy 
2 icy
3 sunny 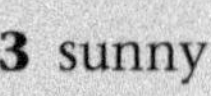
4 raining
5 windy 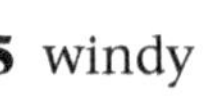
6 hot
7 cold
8 snowing

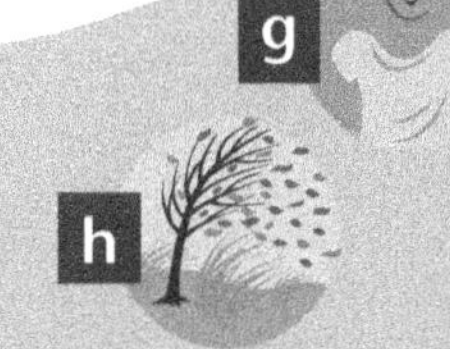

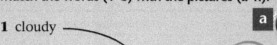

5 Look at the weather map and write sentences. What's the weather like in each country?

Poland: *It's cold and raining in Poland.*
1 Sweden: ....
2 Denmark: ....
3 France: ....
4 Germany: ....
5 Austria: ....
6 Italy: ....

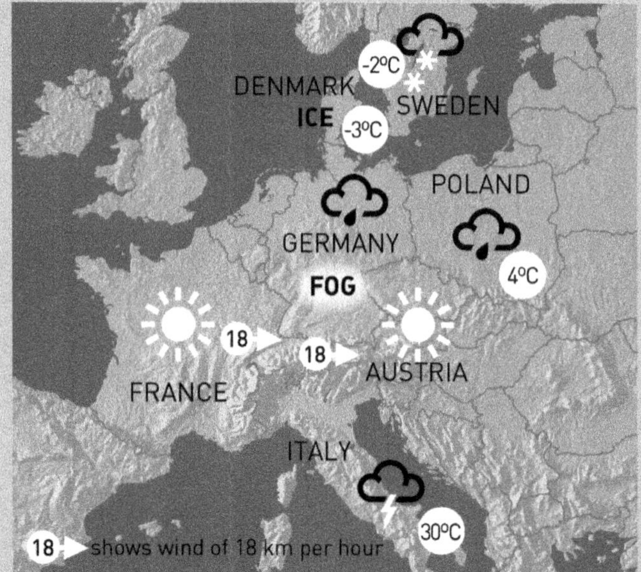

Grammar: present continuous

6 Complete the positive and negative sentences with the words in the box.

are	aren't	~~isn't~~	'm	'm not
's	're	isn't		

It *isn't* raining today. (✗)

1 Outside, the birds .... singing. (✔)
2 I .... sitting at my desk. (✔)
3 The teacher .... talking. (✗)
4 He .... cleaning the board. (✔)
5 The students .... writing in their books. (✗)
6 I .... looking out of the window. (✗)
7 We .... listening to a CD. (✔)

7 Complete the story. Write the present continuous form of the verbs in brackets.

Hi Sarah.
I *'m sitting* (sit) in the park. I
1 .... (watch) some children.
They 2 .... (play) football on the grass. I think they're about 7 or 8 years old. Anyway, I want to talk to you about the party on Saturday. Can you come?
Hang on a minute, Sarah. Oh dear! The ball 3 .... (go) into the road!
The children 4 .... (run) out of the park and they 5 .... (not look) at the road. Oh no! A car 6 .... (come)! It 7 .... (not go) very fast. It's OK. The driver 8 .... (stop) the car. She 9 .... (wait) for one of the boys to get the ball. Good. He's got it!
The kids are all back in the park now.
Sarah? Are you still there? Sorry about that. Now, about the party …

Grammar: present continuous questions

8 Put the words in the correct order to make questions about the story in Exercise 7. Write the short answers.

standing / is / a / shop / Sarah / in / ?
Is Sarah standing in a shop? No, she isn't.

1 a / she / reading / is / newspaper / ?
....
2 football / the / are / playing / children / ?
....
3 lake / the / is / ball / into / going / the / ?
....
4 is / car / a / coming / ?
....
5 it / fast / is / going / ?
....
6 in / the / are / park / children / waiting / the / ?
....

9 Write a sentence for each picture. Use the present continuous form of the verbs.

driver / turn on / car lights
The driver is turning on his car lights.

1 people / put up / umbrellas
....
....

2 boy / take off / jumper
....
....

3 people / hold on to / hats
....
....

4 man / put on / sun cream
....
....

5 girls / put on / gloves
....
....

2B Working in Mongolia

1 ....

Hello. I'm Kelly. I'm a weather forecaster. I do the afternoon weather reports on TV. So, let me tell you about a typical day.

2 ....

I start work at 11 o'clock in the morning. First, I read the information from the weather scientists and then I decide what the weather story is. Today's story is about the snowstorms in Britain. At the moment, it's very windy and it's snowing a lot. In the morning, I usually go to a meeting with the producer and other meteorologists. Together, we decide which graphics to use. Today, I'm showing a satellite picture of the snow clouds and a temperature chart.

Reading and listening

1 **2.1 Read and listen to the weather reporter. Choose the correct picture (a or b) for today's weather.**

2 **Read and listen to the text again. Choose the best heading (a–e) for each paragraph (1–4). There is one extra heading.**

a In the studio
b A busy morning
c My job
d The afternoon
e An early start

3 **Choose the correct answer (a, b or c).**

1 Who decides what the weather story is?
- **a** The producer
- **b** Kelly
- **c** The weather scientists

2 Who chooses the graphics for the weather report?
- **a** everybody
- **b** Kelly and her producer
- **c** Kelly and other meteorologists

3 Who controls the camera in the studio?
- **a** The news director
- **b** Kelly
- **c** The cameraman

4 Where does Kelly do the weather report?
- **a** She usually does the report outside.
- **b** She always does the report inside.
- **c** She sometimes does the report outside.

Grammar: present simple and present continuous

4 **Read these sentences from the text about Kelly. Write *now, today* or *usually*.**

I start work at 11 o'clock in the morning. *usually*
1 First, I read the information from the weather scientists.
2 It's very windy and it's snowing a lot.
3 I go to a meeting with the producer and other meteorologists.
4 I'm showing a satellite picture of the snow clouds.
5 I put a small earpiece in my ear.

5 **Choose the correct form of the verb.**

Kelly *works* / *is working* in a TV studio.
1 She *talks* / *is talking* about her job.
2 She *is starting* / *starts* work at 11 o'clock.
3 She *goes* / *is going to* a meeting every morning.
4 She *is showing* / *shows* a temperature chart today.
5 It often *rains* / *is raining* in Britain.

3 ....

OK. Let's go into the weather studio. As you can see, there aren't any people here. There's just a big blue screen and a camera. When I enter the studio I put on the lights and the microphone. Now look at the camera. I move it up and down by pressing this button here. I also put this small earpiece in my ear so that I can hear the news director who counts me in. You know, '3-2-1, you're on the air!' That means the cameras are recording live. Sometimes I go outside with a cameraman to do the report.

4 ....

In the afternoon, I look at new information and sometimes change the charts. After lunch, I do seven more weather reports and I finish work about 11 o'clock at night. It's a very long day but it's a great job.

6 Look at picture (a) in Exercise 1. Complete the description with the correct form of the verbs in brackets.

Today, the weather *is* (be) cloudy and cold. On the weather chart, it [1] .... (snow) in the north of Britain. The weather reporter [2] .... (stand) outside the studio. She [3] .... (wear) gloves and a scarf. It [4] .... (not snow) at the moment, but there [5] .... (be) snow on the ground.

Working with words: verb + *er* noun

7 a Look at these verbs and find the nouns in the text about Kelly.

verb	noun
report	*reporter*
produce	....
forecast	....

b Now make nouns from these verbs.

verb	noun
farm	....
write	....
drive	....
wait	....
build	....
work	....

8 Match (1–6) with (a–f) to make complete sentences.

1 The train's leaving. Let's get	**a** on the light, please?
2 Please come in and take	**b** off your mobile in the cinema.
3 Can you turn	**c** Let's put on a CD.
4 The sun's very hot. Put	**d** on quickly!
5 Remember to turn	**e** off your coats.
6 I'd like some music.	**f** on some sun cream.

9 Complete each sentence with a verb and *on* or *off*.

I don't like sitting at the front of the plane. So I always *get on* at the back.

1 In Scandinavian homes, people .... their shoes at the door.

2 The streets are very icy. .... some warm boots when you go out.

3 I always forget to .... my mobile again when I leave the cinema.

4 It's bedtime, children. No more stories and .... the lights!

5 Please .... that music! I'm trying to sleep!

6 Look, children! Here's the bus. Wait for the people to .... first.

Study skills: using a dictionary

10 Look at the underlined words. Are they adjectives, nouns or verbs? Check in your dictionary.

1 The weather is <u>cold</u> today.

2 There's <u>snow</u> on the ground.

3 It's <u>icy</u> outside.

4 I've got a <u>cold</u>.

5 I live in a <u>small</u> town.

6 I <u>love</u> listening to live music.

2C Phone messages

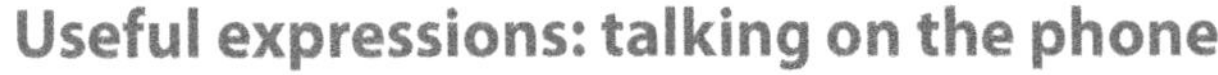

Useful expressions: talking on the phone

1 Match the expressions (1–6) with the correct response (a–f).

1 Hi. Is Leticia there, please?	**a** Yes, please.
2 Who's calling?	**b** Yes. Hang on. I'm looking for a pen.
3 Do you want to leave a message?	**c** Bye.
4 Can I leave a message?	**d** It's the Multi-cinema in Millstown.
5 Can you repeat the name of the cinema?	**e** No, I'm sorry. She's out at the moment.
6 OK. Bye.	**f** It's Danny.

2 Complete the telephone conversation. Use the words in the box.

leave	meet	on	that's	message	repeat	calling	~~there~~

Denzel: Hi. Is Emily *there*, please?
Emily's dad: Who's [1] ....?
Denzel: It's Denzel.
Emily's dad: Oh hello, Denzel. Actually, I think Emily's out at the moment.
Denzel: Oh, can I [2] .... a message?
Emily's dad: Of course. Hang [3] .... I'm just looking for a pen. OK. I've got one.
Denzel: I've got tickets for the Halloween Magic Show tomorrow night. It starts at eight o'clock but we're meeting Leila at half past seven at the clock tower.
Emily's dad: OK. Can you [4] .... the time you're meeting?
Denzel: Half past seven.
Emily's dad: So, that's [5] .... at the clock tower at half past seven. Magic Show starts at eight.
Denzel: Yes, [6] .... right.
Emily's dad: OK. I can give her the [7] .... tonight.
Denzel: Great! Thanks, Mr Anderson. Bye!
Emily's dad: Bye!

Halloween
Magic Show
25-31 October
Royal Theatre

3 Complete the message Emily's dad wrote.

Emily,
Denzel phoned. He's got tickets for the Magic Show .... night. It starts at .... Meet at the .... at seven thirty. .... is going, too.
Dad.

4 2.2 **Listen to two phone calls and complete the messages below. (Use the 'you' form).**

1 From: Emily For: .... Message:	2 From: .... For: Emily Message: ....

5 **Read the phone messages (a–g) and put them in the correct order.**

a
for: Sally,
from: Jake
message: Jake called – they're going to eat in a burger bar or something. He's going to bed now, so don't phone. Don't forget to meet tomorrow at 8 a.m. at his house.
Mum
PS. message from me – don't forget your sun cream!

b
Jake,
Phone Sally when you get back from football. She wants to go to the beach with you tomorrow. What time are you meeting?
Dad

c
Jake,
Sally phoned you back at lunchtime. Phone her this afternoon before she goes to band practice at 5 p.m.
Mum

d
for: Sally
from: Jake
message: He phoned this morning - phone him back at lunchtime.

e
for: Sally
from: Jake
message:
They're catching the bus to the beach at 8.30 in the morning, so meet at his house at 8 a.m.!

f
Jake,
Sally phoned again at about 8 p.m.
Does she need to bring sandwiches or are you buying something to eat there?
Mum

g
for: Sally
from: Jake
message: Jake phoned again just after 5 p.m. He's going to the beach tomorrow. Do you want to go? He needs to know before tonight!
Mum
PS He's got football training this evening from 6 'til 8.

Correct order:
1 *d* **2** **3** **4** **5** **6** **7**

Pronunciation: syllable stress

6 2.3 **Listen to the words and write them in the correct column in the table. Mark the stressed syllable.**

weather sunny tonight outside today icy
waiter police message repeat forget

● •	• ●
....	....
....	....
....	....
....	....
....	....
....	....

Writing: describing a person

7 **Match the description to the correct photo (a or b).**

This is my dad, Bill. He's an art teacher. He loves making things with wood. He makes furniture and toys. He also likes mending things. He spends hours in the garage every weekend. In this picture, he's making a toy for my little cousin. His toys are fantastic and he sometimes sells them, but he usually gives them to people as presents. He's also making my brother a tree house in the garden.

a

8 **Write a description of the second photo.**

This / my grandfather
work / hospital
love / his garden
grow / vegetables
spend a lot of time / his grandchildren
In this picture, play in the garden / my little brother, Owen.

b

2D Explore more

Reading

1 **Look again at this picture of Kelly. Read description (a) below. Highlight the correct information. Highlight the incorrect information in a different colour.**

a In the picture, there's a weather chart showing very hot, sunny weather. A weather reporter is talking about the weather. She's standing in front of the weather chart in the studio. She's wearing a grey jacket.

2 **Read these two descriptions of the picture. Highlight the correct and incorrect information in the texts. Then circle the correct description (b or c).**

b In the picture, the weather reporter is talking about the weather in Britain. It's cloudy and raining. She's standing outside. She's wearing a grey jacket and she's looking at the weather chart.

c In the picture, a TV weather reporter is standing outside. She's wearing a grey jacket. It's raining and she's holding an umbrella. She's looking into the camera and talking about the weather on the chart.

3 **Choose the best description (a, b or c) for the photo.**

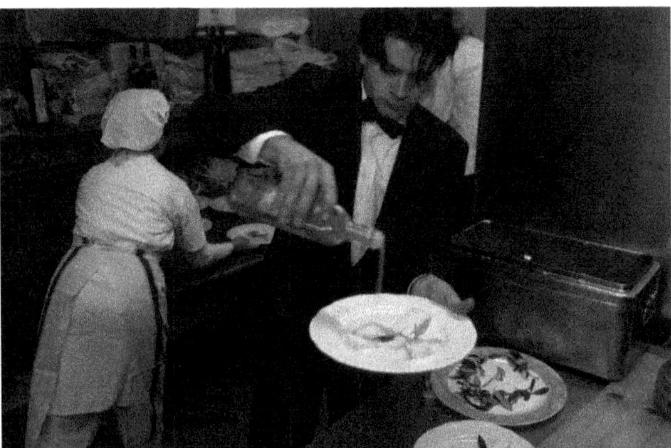

a In the photo, I can see two people working in a kitchen. A girl is putting food on a plate. She's wearing a white hat. There's a waiter in front of her. He's carrying three plates of food. He's wearing a black jacket and trousers and a white shirt.

b In the photo, there's a waiter. He's putting oil on some food. There's a girl behind him. She's wearing a white hat and she's putting plates of food on a table. The waiter is wearing a black jacket and a white shirt.

c In the photo, I can see people working in a kitchen. A cook is putting oil on some food. She's wearing a white hat. A waiter is carrying dirty plates into the kitchen. He's wearing a black jacket and a white shirt.

Listening

4 2.2 **Listen to the dialogue. Choose the correct picture (a, b or c).**

a

b

c

5 2.5 **Listen to three dialogues. Match each dialogue (1–3) with one of the pictures (a–e). There are two extra pictures. You can listen to the dialogues twice.**

Dialogue 1	....
Dialogue 2	....
Dialogue 3	....

a

b

c

d

e

Word list Unit 2

(a) bit (n) ....
area (n) ....
autumn (n) ....
bar (n) ....
bear (n) ....
bear cub (n) ....
because (conj) ....
bedtime (n) ....
below (prep) ....
belt (n) ....
behaviour (n) ....
blanket (n) ....
border (n) ....
bounce (v) ....
box (n) ....
bring (v) ....
build (v) ....
can (modal v) ....
carry (v) ....
catch (v) ....
chart (n) ....
clean (adj) ....
cloudy (adj) ....
coast (n) ....
coat (n) ....
crystal (n) ....
customer (n) ....
dangerous (adj) ....
direction (n) ....
drum (n) ....
during (prep) ....
earpiece (n) ....
enter (v) ....
equipped (adj) ....
erupt (v) ....
experiment (n) ....
face (n) ....
fly (v) ....
foggy (adj) ....
forecast (v) ....
furniture (n) ....
get off (phr v) ....
get on (phr v) ....
give advice (phr) ....
glove (n) ....
go out (phr v) ....
ground (n) ....
hang on (phr v) ....
happen (v) ....
hold on (phr v) ....
hunter (n) ....
icy (adj) ....
illness (n) ....
in the field (phr) ....
in the path of (phr) ....
inside (prep) ....
keep (v) ....
lake (n) ....
lava (n) ....
liquid (n) ....
look out (phr v) ....
lorry (n) ....
magma (n) ....
mark (n) ....
meal (n) ....
measure (n) ....
mend (v) ....
moose (n) ....
move (v) ....
outside (prep) ....
ox (*pl* oxen) (n) ....
plate (n) ....
population (n) ....
predict (v) ....
pressure (n) ....
probe (v) ....
put on (phr v) ....
put up (phr v) ....
quiet (adj) ....
record (n) ....
repeat (v) ....
ride (v) ....
salt (n) ....
scary (adj) ....
scientist (n) ....
sculpture (n) ....
serve (v) ....
shape (n) ....
size (n) ....
ski (v) ....
sky (n) ....
snowflake (n) ....
solid (adj) ....
steam (n) ....
stormy (adj) ....
stretch (v) ....
suitcase (n) ....
sunny (adj) ....
take off (phr v) ....
tent (n) ....
thermal suit (n) ....
throat (n) ....
tidy (n) ....
tiny (adj) ....
tower (n) ....
tracking device (n) ....
travel (v) ....
trip (n) ....
truck (n) ....
turn off (phr v) ....
turn on (phr v) ....
umbrella (n) ....
wait (v) ....
watch out (phr v) ....
weather (n) ....
wild (adj) ....
wind (n) ....
windy (adj) ....
wolf (*pl* wolves) (n) ....
wood (n) ....

U2 Reading Explorer

behaviour (n) ....
equipped (adj) ....
erupt (v) ....
give advice (phr) ....
in the field (phr) ....
in the path of (phr) ....
lava (n) ....
magma (n) ....
pressure (n) ....
probe (v) ....
steam (n) ....
thermal suit (n) ....
tracking device (n) ....

Grammar Practice Unit 2

Present continuous

We use **present continuous** to talk about actions that are happening now, at or around the moment when we speak. We form the present continuous with ***am***, ***are*** or ***is*** and the main verb with ***-ing***.

*Quiet, please! **I'm** trying to do my homework.*

*We **are** learning about hurricanes in today's lesson.*

*Oh no! **It's** raining again!*

With verbs ending in a **consonant + *-e***, we change the ***-e*** to ***-ing***.

chase chas**ing** dance danc**ing**

With most verbs ending in a **single vowel + a consonant**, we double the consonant and add ***-ing***.

win win**ning** get get**ting**

With verbs ending in ***-ie***, we change the ***-ie*** to ***-ying***.

lie **lying** die **dying**

We form the negative by adding the word ***not*** after ***am/are/is***. The short forms are the same as for the verb ***be***.

***I'm not** feeling very well.*

*You **aren't** listening!*

*It's cold, but it **isn't** snowing.*

Affirmative		
I'm	(I am)	
You're/We're/They're	(You/We/They are)	reading now.
He's/She's/It's	(He/She/It is)	
Negative		
I'm not (I am not)		
You/We/They aren't (are not)		reading now.
He/She/It isn't (is not)		

1 Complete the affirmative (✔) and negative (✘) sentences with the verb *be*. Use short forms.

It's raining hard and it's very windy. ✔

1. We .... swimming now, because the water's a bit cold. ✘
2. I .... waiting for the rain to stop. ✔
3. It's very cold, but he .... wearing a jumper. ✘
4. They .... practising for the school concert. ✔
5. No, I .... having lunch now – it's only eleven o'clock! ✘
6. You .... playing really well today! ✔

2 Complete the sentences with the present continuous form of the verbs in brackets. Use short forms.

I'm looking out of the window at the storm. (**look**)

1. You don't need your umbrella. It .... now. (**not rain**)
2. Look, Mum – we .... a pizza in the microwave. (**cook**)
3. I can't play with you now – I .... my homework. (**do**)
4. Kate and Judy aren't here – they .... in the park. (**walk**)
5. 'Where's Jamie?' 'I think he .... TV.' (**watch**)
6. You .... me study by talking to me, you know. (**not help**)

3 Complete the sentences with the present continuous form of the verbs in brackets.

These plants *are dying* because they haven't got any water. (**die**)

1. He .... off his jumper because he's hot. (**take**)
2. The sun .... but it's very warm. (**not shine**)
3. Hi – we're in Spain, and we .... a great time! (**have**)
4. Great! The rain .... at last! (**stop**)
5. I .... on my bed and listening to music. (**lie**)
6. They .... their gloves on because they're cold. (**put**)

4 Write negative (✘) and affirmative (✔) sentences in the present continuous. Use short forms.

It / rain / now ✘ It / snow ✔

It isn't raining now. It's snowing.

1. I / talk / on my mobile ✘ I / send / a text message ✔

   ....

2. You / do / your homework ✘ You / watch / TV ✔

   ....

3. Sophie / dance / now ✘ She / have / a rest ✔

   ....

4. We / study / right now ✘ We / write / emails ✔

   ....

5. Will / practise the drums ✘ He / meet / his friends ✔

   ....

6. Adam and Lewis / lie / on the sofa ✘ They / sit / on the rug ✔

   ....

We make questions in present continuous by putting ***Am/Are/Is*** before the subject, and then the main verb with ***-ing***.

We can use ***Wh-*** question words at the beginning of the sentence.

***Am** I **making** a lot of noise?*

*What **are** you **looking** at?*

***Is** it **snowing** in your town today?*

In short answers we use ***am/'m not, are/aren't*** or ***is/isn't***. We DON'T use the main verb.

5 Complete these questions with *am, is* or *are*.

Are you feeling a bit hungry? I am!

1 .... I holding this violin the right way?

2 .... he helping his dad in the garden?

3 What .... we waiting for?

4 .... you talking to me?

5 Why .... she putting on her gloves?

6 Put the words into the correct order to make questions.

packing / you / are / your suitcase / ?

Are you packing your suitcase?

1 Will / is / thinking / about school / ?

....

2 Judy and Kate / about me / are / talking / ?

....

3 flying / Rebecca / into a hurricane / is / ?

....

4 in the city / raining / at the moment / it / is / ?

....

5 are / waiting / for someone / you and Lewis / ?

....

7 Now write affirmative (✔) or negative (✘) short answers to the questions in Exercise 6.

(Are you packing your suitcase?) (✔) *Yes, I am.*

1 (✘) .... **4** (✘) ....

2 (✔) .... **5** (✘) ....

3 (✔) ....

8 Write questions in the present continuous. Then write short answers and affirmative sentences.

Will / do / his homework? No – he / practise / the drums

Is Will doing his homework? No, he isn't. He's practising the drums.

you / help / your mother? Yes – I / tidy / my bedroom

Are you helping your mother? Yes, I am. I'm tidying my bedroom.

1 you / write / a story? No – I / make / a shopping list

....

2 Kate / talk / to Lewis? No – she / leave / a message for him

....

3 they / sit / in the park? Yes – they / listen / to the birds singing

....

4 you / look / for something? Yes – we / try / to find Kate's mobile

....

Present simple and present continuous

We use the **present simple** to talk about things that someone ***usually (often/always/etc)*** does, and we use the **present continuous** to talk about actions that are happening **now**, at or around the time when we are talking.

*Fran usually **lives** in Rome.*

*She's **living** in Paris at the moment.*

*My dad **works** in a shop.*

*He **isn't working** today – it's Sunday.*

9 Choose the correct words to complete the conversation.

A: My dad's a pilot. He *flies* / ~~*is flying*~~ planes.

B: Really? [1] *Does he sometimes fly / Is he sometimes flying* to Madrid?

A: Yes, [2] *he does / he is*. He [3] *often goes / is often going* to Madrid.

B: [4] *Does he fly / Is he flying* there right now?

A: No, [5] *he doesn't / he isn't*. I think [6] *he sleeps / he's sleeping* right now.

B: [7] *Doesn't he work / Isn't he working* today then?

A: I don't know, but he [8] *usually flies / is usually flying* at night.

10 Write sentences in present simple or present continuous using the words and phrase in brackets.

We / wear / a school uniform (usually)

We usually wear a school uniform.

We / wear / ordinary clothes (today)

We're wearing ordinary clothes today.

1 Kate and Judy / meet / their friends after school (often)

2 It / rain / very hard here (at the moment)

3 Will / practise / the drums in the evening (usually)

4 I / send / you an email (right now)

5 Jamie / be / late for school (sometimes)

Review Units 1 and 2

1 Write *a, an, the* or – (no article).

1 My dad's got .... blue car.
2 She's wearing .... jacket.
3 .... sea is very blue today.
4 What time do you start .... school?
5 I've got .... aunt in New Zealand.
6 Do you like .... new maths teacher?
7 My mother has .... breakfast in bed every Sunday.
8 My sister's favourite film is .... *Matrix*.
9 .... Notting Hill Carnival is in August.
10 Don't look at .... sun! It's dangerous!

1 mark per item: ... / 10 marks

2 Choose the correct adverb of frequency.

1 It almost *often / never* rains in the desert.
2 It is *sometimes / always* sunny in Antarctica.
3 Buses are *never / sometimes* late.
4 People *often / never* swim in the sea in summer.
5 It *never / usually* snows in Russia in winter.

1 mark per item: ... / 5 marks

3 Rewrite the sentences using the verb and a suitable adverb (*always, often, usually, sometimes, never*).

We have eggs for breakfast every Sunday.
We always have eggs for breakfast on Sundays.

1 I watch TV four or five times a week.
I .... TV.
2 I tidy my bedroom every day.
I .... my bedroom.
3 My dad makes the dinner once a week.
My dad .... the dinner.
4 Me and my brother walk to school, except when it rains.
We .... to school.
5 My mum does all the housework. We don't help.
We .... my mum with the housework.

2 marks per item: ... / 10 marks

4 Choose the correct verb form to complete the sentences.

1 I *go / goes / going* to a theatre group after school.
2 We *performs / performing / perform* a play every year.
3 I love *be / am / being* in the play.
4 Our teacher *be / is / are* a brilliant actor.
5 He doesn't *likes / like / liking* wearing make-up.

1 mark per item: ... / 5 marks

5 Complete the dialogue. Write the correct form of the verbs in brackets.

Paul: Do you [1] .... (have) a lot of hobbies?
Linda: Yes, I [2] .... (do). I love [3] .... (play) tennis and volleyball. I also like [4] .... (make) things. What about you?
Paul: I love [5] .... (paint) and I [6] .... (go) to an art club every Tuesday.
Linda: Really? I [7] .... (not like) art. It's boring.
Paul: No, it [8] .... (not be)! At the art club, we [9] .... (make) lots of things, too. Why don't you [10] .... (come) next week?
Linda: OK. What time?

1 mark per item: ... / 10 marks

6 Complete the sentences and questions with verbs in the correct form.

1 I usually .... swimming on Sundays.
2 .... Max have a lot of hobbies?
3 He often .... chess with his dad.
4 A: .... Julie in her bedroom?
B: Yes, she is. She .... to music.
5 The shops .... at 9 o'clock every morning.
6 A: The students are in the library.
B: Are they .... their homework?
7 A: You look different. Are you .... make-up?
B: Yes, I am. I .... in the school play this afternoon.
8 My friends .... in the school choir every lunchtime.

1 mark per item: ... / 10 marks

7 Circle the odd one out.

1 comics books chess
2 art pop hip hop
3 clothes shoes cycling
4 cinema drawing painting
5 violin drums skateboarding
6 dancing animals singing
7 tidying your bedroom doing the housework playing football
8 studying playing computer games doing homework

1 mark per item: … / 8 marks

8 Write the missing words.

1 I'm dancing in the end-of-year s.............................. at school.
2 My friends are acting in a p.............................. at the theatre.
3 I can play two i.............................. : the piano and the flute.
4 My sister s.............................. in a rock band.
5 I love the c............................... The acrobats are my favourite.
6 Good musicians p.............................. for many hours every day.
7 My class are taking p.............................. in the music festival this year.

1 mark per item: … / 7 marks

9 Write the weather words.

1

It's c.............................. and r..............................

2

It's very h.............................. and s...............................

3
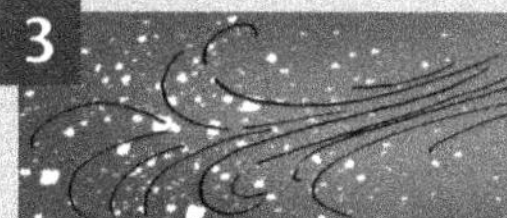
It's s.............................. and it's very w..............................

4
It's very s.............................. and there's a t.............................. coming!

5
It's f.............................. and i.............................. tonight.

1 mark per item: … / 10 marks

10 Complete the definitions with the words in the box.

animals	hospital	lorry	news	telephone

1 A nurse works in a(n) ....
2 A vet works with ....
3 A reporter writes about the ....
4 A truck driver spends a lot of time in a ....
5 A receptionist answers the ....

1 mark per item: … / 5 marks

11 Write the jobs.

1 A .... predicts the weather.
2 A .... produces vegetables or meat.
3 A .... helps people to learn.
4 A .... does scientific experiments.
5 A .... serves people in a shop.

2 marks per item: … / 10 marks

12 Complete the sentences with *off, on* or *up*.

1 It's cold now. I want to put .... my jacket.
2 Don't forget to take .... your shoes before you go in the house.
3 Turn .... the TV. I want to watch the news.
4 I'm getting .... the bus now. This is my stop.
5 Remember to turn .... your mobile phone in the cinema.
6 The train's leaving in a minute. Let's get .... quickly!
7 Let's put some music ....! Do you like hip hop?
8 It's getting dark. Can you put the light ...., please?
9 It's raining! Why don't you put your umbrella ....?
10 Come in and take your coats .... Would you like some tea?

1 mark per item: … / 10 marks

Total marks: … / 100

3A The history of writing

Vocabulary: mass media

1 Write the words under each picture.

1 the I.......................... **2** a D.......................... **3** a b.......................... **4** an e..........................

5 a b.......................... **6** a r....... pr.......

2 Complete the text with the words from Exercise 1. Put the words in the plural form where necessary.

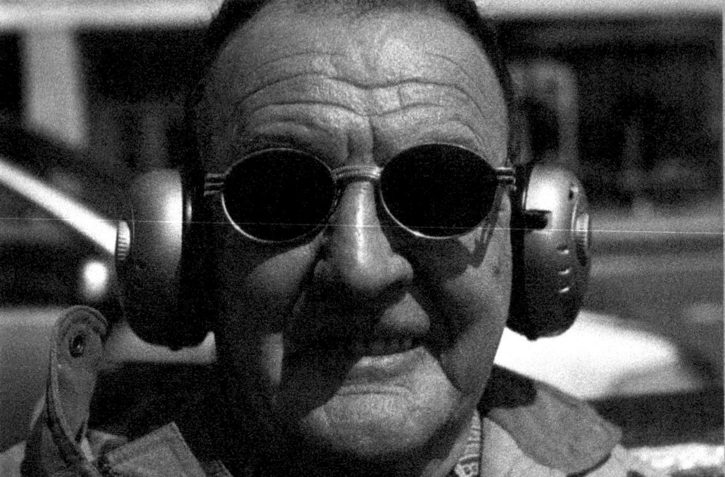

My grandfather hasn't got an iPod and he doesn't watch *podcasts*. But he uses the [1] .... every day. He's a musician in a band. He sends [2] .... and he's even got a [3] .... where he writes about the band. He doesn't use the computer for anything else. He still listens to his favourite [4] .... on his old radio and buys [5] .... of his favourite films.

3 Complete the text with the correct form of the verbs in the box.

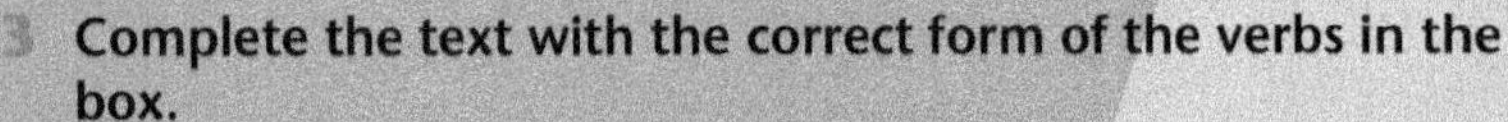

listen	read (x2)	send (x2)	take	use	watch

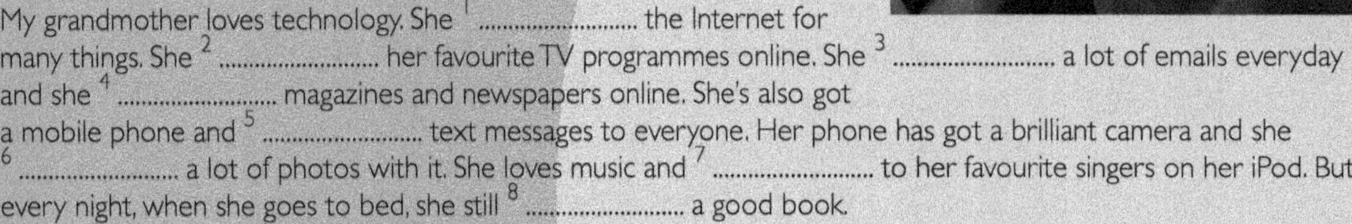

My grandmother loves technology. She [1] .... the Internet for many things. She [2] .... her favourite TV programmes online. She [3] .... a lot of emails everyday and she [4] .... magazines and newspapers online. She's also got a mobile phone and [5] .... text messages to everyone. Her phone has got a brilliant camera and she [6] .... a lot of photos with it. She loves music and [7] .... to her favourite singers on her iPod. But every night, when she goes to bed, she still [8] .... a good book.

Grammar: *was* and *were*

4 Complete the dialogue with *was, wasn't, were* or *weren't*.

A: Hello, Matilda. Where [1] .... you last night? You [2] .... at the gym, as usual.

B: No, that's true. I [3] .... there last night. I [4] .... at the première of the new Bond film. It [5] .... fantastic!

A: [6] .... you, really? Which famous actors [7] .... there?

B: Well, Daniel Craig [8] .... there, of course, and lots of other celebrities [9] .... there, too.

A: What about Pierce Brosnan? I think he [10] .... the best James Bond.

B: He's my favourite Bond, too, but I'm afraid he [11] .... there.

A: Oh. That's a pity. Next time, perhaps.

Grammar: regular and irregular verbs

5 Complete the sentences with the past simple form of the verbs in brackets.

I didn't watch television last night. (not watch)

1 I .... an interesting book about the Pharaohs last week. (read)

2 I .... an email to my cousin in Australia yesterday and I .... a reply this morning! (write, receive)

3 Last night, I .... to some music on my MP3 player and .... some text messages. (listen, send)

4 The film .... at eight o'clock and .... at half past nine. (begin, end)

5 Yesterday, in the history class, we .... a lot about the Egyptians. (learn)

6 In my first year at primary school, I .... the teacher and I.......................... to him for six months! (not like, not speak)

6 Read the extracts (a–g) from the story of the history of printing. Complete the text with the correct past form of the verbs in brackets.

7 Put the paragraphs (a–g) from the story of the history of printing in the correct order (1–7).

1 ..C.. **2** .... **3** .... **4** .... **5** .... **6** .... **7** ....

Working with words: *in, ago, last*

8 Complete the sentences with *in, ago* or *last.*

1 I bought a new dress .... week.

2 My dad started a new job two weeks ....

3 There was a great film on TV .... night.

4 People didn't have computers .... the nineteenth century.

5 My grandparents got married .... 1962.

6 Two years ...., my best friend moved to America.

7 My sister went to university .... September.

A SHORT HISTORY OF PRINTING

a Later, Koenig and Bauer *developed* (develop) a machine which [1] .... (print) on both sides of the paper at the same time. Newspapers and booksellers [2] .... (begin) to sell thousands of copies.

b In the 1450s, Johann Gutenberg [3] .... (invent) the first printing press. The printer [4] .... (put) each sheet of paper into the machine by hand.

c In the 13th century, monks [5] .... (copy) books by hand. It [6] .... (take) about one year to copy the Bible.

d The printing press [7] .... (not change) for three hundred years. Then, in 1812, Koenig and Bauer [8] .... (use) steam power to develop a new machine which [9] .... (make) tens of thousands of copies of a page in one day.

e The monks [10] .... (have) beautiful handwriting (calligraphy) and they [11] .... (decorate) the pages with colourful illustrations.

f In 1843, an American called Richard M. Hoe [12] .... (design) the rotary press. The machine [13] .... (print) on continuous sheets of paper and [14] .... (produce) millions of copies a day.

g In Europe, many rich and important people, including the Pope, [15] .... (think) that Gutenberg's machine [16] .... (be) a bad idea. They [17] .... (not want) printed books in their libraries.

3B Blockbusters

Vocabulary: films

1 Choose the correct option.

The Matrix is a *science fiction film* / *cartoon* starring Keanu Reeves.

1 *Harry Potter and the Sorcerer's Stone* is *a fantasy film* / *a horror film.*

2 *Mamma Mia* is a brilliant *cartoon* / *musical.*

3 I love the films of Miyazaki. They are *Japanese cartoons* / *American action films* and they're fantastic!

4 I don't like watching *horror films* / *comedy films* – they're too frightening.

5 I don't usually enjoy *romance* / *science fiction* films but *You've Got Mail* was very good.

Reading

2 Read the text and match the questions (1 and 2) with the answers (a and b).

1 How much did it cost to make the series?

2 How many people watched the first episode?

a 6 million

b over £3 million

LONDONERS

THE POLISH TV SOAP OPERA SET IN LONDON

The Polish TV channel, TVP1, showed the first episode of *Londoners* on October 23rd, 2008.

Six million people watched the first episode of the new soap opera. Before the first episode there were lots of posters for the TV show. Radio stations in Poland and in England had competitions to win a part in the show.

The new *TV series cost 13.5 million złoty (£3.3 million). The dialogues are in English and Polish. The production company, Twilight Films, filmed indoor scenes in studios in Poland but they spent a lot of money on filming outside in London. For the first series they used interesting locations such as the London Eye and Wembley stadium.

Londoners is about Polish people who live in London. There are two famous actors in the series. Robert Więckiewicz plays Marcin and Grażyna Barszczewska plays Nina. Marcin is a history teacher in his forties but he can't get a job in London. He has a wife and a son. Nina is a woman who left Poland in the 1940s. Now she rents rooms to new Polish immigrants.

The stories in the new soap opera are based on real people. Before they wrote the episodes, the writers talked to Polish people in London who told them about their experiences.

*TV series = soap opera or drama with lots of episodes

3 Read the text again and answer the questions.

1 When was the first episode of *Londoners* shown?

2 What was Marcin's job in Poland?

3 When did Nina go to London?

4 What did radio stations in England and Poland do?

5 Who did the writers talk to?

Listening

4 3.1 **Listen. What did Danny watch last night? Choose the correct answer (a, b or c).**

a *Londoners*
b *Prison Break*
c a DVD of *Prison Break*

5 **Listen again and choose the correct answer (a, b or c).**

1 Who watched *Londoners* last night?
a Danny **b** Amy **c** Amy's mum

2 Amy said that *Londoners* was:
a interesting **b** boring **c** exciting

3 What was Danny's opinion of *Londoners*?
a It was boring. **b** It was interesting.
c It was OK.

4 What did Danny do last night?
a He watched a DVD.
b He watched TV with his mum.
c He went to bed early.

5 Did Amy like the first series of *Prison Break*?
a She didn't watch it. **b** No, she didn't.
c Yes, she did.

6 When did Danny go to bed?
a He went to bed early.
b He went to bed very late.
c He went to bed at 11 p.m.

Working with words: adjectives with -ed or -ing

6 **Choose the correct adjective to complete the dialogues.**

1
A: The producers of *Londoners* filmed scenes in *interesting / interested* places in London.
B: Yes, but I was *surprising / surprised* that they also used studios in Poland.

2
A: The special effects in *The Matrix* were *amazed / amazing.*
B: I agree, but the story was *confusing / confused.*

3
A: Did you see *Cirque du Soleil* on TV last night? It was really *exciting / excited.*
B: Yes, I did. The acrobats were fantastic. I was really *amazing / amazed.*

4
A: I watched a horror film on DVD with my brother last night.
B: Was it good? Were you very *frightened / frightening?*
A: Not really. I didn't understand the story, and it was so long that it was very *tiring / tired* to watch!

Grammar: past simple question forms

7 **Put the words in the correct order to make questions.**

TV / you / night / last / did / watch / ?
Did you watch TV last night?

1 you / watch / did / *Cirque du Soleil* / ?

....

2 enjoy / you / it / did / ?

....

3 were / who / your / performers / favourite / ?

....

4 it / what / did / finish / time / ?

....

5 your / watch / parents / it / did / ?

....

8 **Match the questions (1–5) from Exercise 7 with the answers (a–e).**

a At eleven thirty.
b No, they didn't. They went to bed.
c The Chinese acrobats.
d Yes. It was brilliant!
e Yes, I did.

3C Agreeing and disagreeing

1 Match (1–6) with (a–f) to form useful expressions.

1 Me	**a** your opinion?
2 I think	**b** think of this film?
3 What do you	**c** with you / with Judy.
4 What's	**d** it's great!
5 I agree	**e** agree.
6 I don't	**f** too!

2 Complete the dialogue with the words in the box.

opinion ~~think~~ don't awful with too way great

Carla: You and Paveł are from Poland, right? What do you *think* of this new soap opera, *Londoners*?

Kasia: I don't like it at all. It's just not real. In fact, I think it's [1] .... !

Carla: Me, [2] .... I watched it on my iPod. It was really boring.

Kasia: Yes. And all the Polish characters are horrible!

Paveł: Sorry, I [3] .... agree. I think it's [4] .... ! My cousins in Poland watch it. They say it's the best programme on TV.

Kasia: No [5] .... ! John, what's your [6] .... ?

John: Actually, I agree [7] .... Paveł. I think it's really good. The characters and stories are interesting.

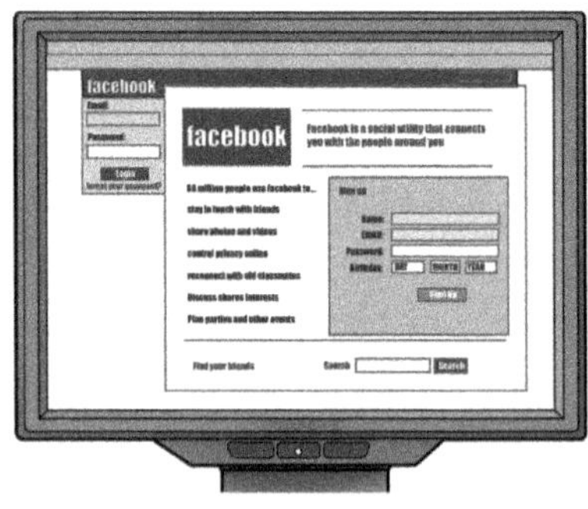

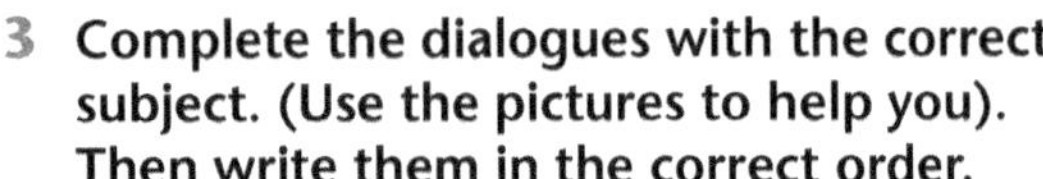

3 Complete the dialogues with the correct subject. (Use the pictures to help you). Then write them in the correct order.

Dialogue 1

Paveł: I think it's great!

John: What do you think of the new ....?

John: What's your opinion, Carla?

Kasia: Me too. I think it's brilliant!

Carla: I don't know. What exactly is an ....?

Correct order

1 *John: What do you think of the new* ....?
2 ....
3 ....
4 ....
5 ....

Dialogue 2

Kasia: No. I don't like it. I think it's a stupid idea!

Paveł: It's OK, but I think it's more for girls.

Carla: Are you on ....?

Carla: Oh. What do you think of it, Paveł?

John: Me too. I agree with Kasia. It's just not cool!

Correct order

1 ....
2 ....
3 ....
4 ....
5 *Pavel: It's OK, but I think it's more for girls.*

Pronunciation: -ed endings

4 3.2 **Listen and repeat the past tense verbs. Write them in the correct column in the table.**

/t/	/d/	/id/
....	*played*	....
....	....	....
....	....	....
....	....	....
....	....	....
....	....	....

~~played~~ enjoyed invented liked looked
painted created watched talked agreed
used helped finished listened lived started

Writing: a blog

5 **Read Danny's blog entry about last weekend. Choose the best title to describe his weekend.**

1 A surprising weekend
2 A typical weekend
3 An exciting weekend

Last weekend wasn't very interesting. It rained all morning on Saturday, so I stayed at home. I tidied my room and helped mum in the kitchen. I cleaned out the fridge! After lunch, I went shopping with my mum. We spent an hour and a half in the supermarket. It was really boring!
Then it stopped raining, so I met Craig in the park. Then Amy, Emily and Karim joined us. We went home about six o'clock but decided to meet tomorrow to play tennis. When I got home, my mum gave me a new sweatshirt. It was OK, which was surprising because my mum usually buys me awful clothes!
In the evening, there were some good comedy programmes on TV, so we all watched them and I went to bed quite early!
Sunday was a very typical day! I got up late, did my homework, took the dog for a walk and then we went to my grandma's for lunch. In the afternoon, I played tennis with the gang and then came home, had tea and looked at some videos on YouTube. In the evening, I watched almost the whole first series of *Prison Break* on DVD and didn't go to bed until really late!

6 **Read the blog again and answer the questions.**

What was the weather like on Saturday morning?
It was raining.

1 Did Danny go out on Saturday morning?
....
2 What housework did he do?
....
3 Where did he go with his mum?
....
4 What did he do when it stopped raining?
....
5 When did he do his homework?
....
6 Who did he play tennis with?
....
7 What did he do on Sunday evening?
....

7 **Look at these two sentences from the blog. Write *but* or *because*, then check with the text.**

1 We went home about six o'clock .... decided to meet tomorrow to play tennis.
2 It was OK, which was surprising .... my mum usually buys me awful clothes!

8 **Make notes about your weekend. Use past tense verbs.**

Saturday: *Stayed at home, played computer games, ...*
Sunday: *Got up late, read the newspaper and some magazines, ...*

....
....
....
....
....
....

Tip! Use linking words and time expressions such as *then, but, because* and *in the afternoon, in the morning, after lunch* etc.

9 **Read your notes and add adjectives of opinion.**

I stayed at home, played ^*boring* *computer games.*

I got up late, read the newspaper and some ^*really interesting* *magazines.*

10 **Now write your blog. Add your photo if you like!**

3D Explore More

1 Read the sentences (a–f) about Danny and put them in a logical order.

a .... When he got home, his mum gave him a new sweatshirt.

b .... Then he went to the park to meet his friends.

c .... He tidied his room and cleaned out the fridge.

d .... He also helped with the supermarket shopping in the afternoon.

e .... Danny liked it. He was surprised because his mum usually buys awful clothes for him.

f .... On Saturday morning, Danny helped his mum with the housework.

2 Now choose the best answer (1, 2 or 3).

1 f, b, a, e, d, c
2 f, c, e, a, d, b
3 f, c, d, b, a, e

3 Put the sentences (a–e) about Amy in a logical order. in order to make a logical text. Choose the correct answer (1, 2 or 3).

Dear Amy,

a It was a girl and she was born at four o'clock in the morning.
b My aunt had a baby last night!
c Thanks for your email the other day about your cousin's birthday party.
d Me and mum went shopping this morning and we bought the baby a cute pink dress!
e I've got some exciting news to tell you.

See you soon,
Jenny

1 c, a, b, e, d
2 c, e, b, a, d
3 c, a, d, b, e

4 Put the sentences in order to make a logical text. Choose the correct answer (1, 2 or 3).

a They fell on houses and on electricity cables.
b Last month, there was a bad storm in Spain.
c Many trees fell down in the wind.
d Some people didn't have electricity for nearly two weeks!
e It rained a lot and was really windy.

1 b, e, c, a, d
2 b, a, d, c, e
3 b, c, e, d, a

5 Choose the correct words from the options below (a, b or c) to complete the dialogue.

Jenny: *Did you visit* your aunt the other day?
Amy: Yes, [1] ....
Jenny: [2] .... did you visit her?
Amy: At her house. She [3] .... the baby at home.
Jenny: Was the baby asleep?
Amy: Yes, she [4] .... at all. It was really boring!

a You visited	**b** Did you visit (circled)	**c** You visit
1 a we visited	**b** we did visit	**c** we did
2 a Where	**b** When	**c** Why
3 a has	**b** had	**c** have
4 a didn't wake up	**b** woke up	**c** not wake up

6 Choose the correct expression from the options below (a, b or c) to complete the text.

Friday, 10 December

[1] .... to school today [2] .... it was closed. [3] .... a lot yesterday and the road to our school [4] .... icy. In the afternoon, the school buses [5] .... School finished early, at 2.30 p.m., and [6] .... home in the snow.

1 a I went	**b** Did I go	**c** I didn't go
2 a because	**b** so	**c** why
3 a Snowed	**b** It snowed	**c** Snow
4 a was	**b** had	**c** did
5 a didn't come	**b** come	**c** not come
6 a we walk	**b** we walked	**c** did we walk

Word list Unit 3

actually (adv)	....
advertisement (advert) (n)	....
agree (with) (v)	....
amazed (adj)	....
amazing (adj)	....
appear (v)	....
around (prep)	....
arrive (v)	....
associate (v)	....
blockbuster (n)	....
bookseller (n)	....
bored (adj)	....
boring (adj)	....
brilliant (adj)	....
broke off (phr v)	....
cartoon (n)	....
cave (n)	....
celebration (n)	....
celebrity (n)	....
clone (v)	....
confused (adj)	....
confusing (adj)	....
connect (v)	....
continuous (adj)	....
create (v)	....
crossed with (phr)	....
cuneiform (adj)	....
cute (adj)	....
decorate (v)	....
design (v)	....
develop (v)	....
direct (v)	....
director (n)	....
discover (v)	....
donkey (n)	....
enjoy (v)	....
episode (n)	....
eventually (adv)	....
evolve (v)	....
exactly (adj)	....
excited (adj)	....
exciting (adj)	....
fall down (phr)	....
fall in love (phr)	....
favourite (adj)	....
freedom (n)	....
fridge (n)	....
frightened (adj)	....
frightening (adj)	....
gift (n)	....
handwriting (n)	....
hometown (n)	....
independence (n)	....
industry (n)	....
interested (adj)	....
interesting (adj)	....
invent (v)	....
island (n)	....
isolated (adj)	....
jaw (n)	....
journey (n)	....
knight (n)	....
mammal (n)	....
middle (prep)	....
middle finger (n)	....
monk (n)	....
ordinary (adj)	....
perhaps (adv)	....
period (n)	....
pharaoh (n)	....
possible (adj)	....
power (n)	....
powerful (adj)	....
prefer (v)	....
print (v)	....
printing machine (n)	....
puma (n)	....
quite (adv)	....
realise (v)	....
receive (v)	....
rent (v)	....
repair (n)	....
reply (v)	....
represent (v)	....
reptile (n)	....
rotary press (n)	....
route (n)	....
sabre (n)	....
sail (v)	....
sign (n)	....
sink (v)	....
snake (n)	....
soap opera (n)	....
sound (n)	....
species (n)	....
steam (adj)	....
stripe (n)	....
subtitle (n)	....
suddenly (adv)	....
super-continent (n)	....
surprising (adj)	....
sweatshirt (n)	....
ticket (n)	....
tired (adj)	....
tiring (adj)	....
topic (n)	....
treasure (n)	....
turn into (phr v)	....
uncle (n)	....
unique (adj)	....
voice (n)	....
voyage (n)	....
whole (adj)	....

U3 Reading Explorer

broke off (phr v)	....
crossed with (phr)	....
evolve (v)	....
isolated (adj)	....
mammal (n)	....
middle finger (n)	....
puma (n)	....
reptile (n)	....
species (n)	....
super-continent (n)	....
unique (adj)	....

Past simple *be*

The **past simple** of the verb ***be*** is ***was*** and ***were***.

*I **was** at the cinema last night.*

*He/She/It **was** the star of the film.*

*You/We/They **were** sad at the end of the movie.*

The negative is ***was not*** (***wasn't***) or ***were not*** (***weren't***).

*I **wasn't** interested in watching the TV show.*

*He/She/It **wasn't** the star of that movie.*

*You/We/They **weren't** born in 1964.*

Affirmative		
I	was	at school this morning.
You/We/They	were	
He/She/It	was	
Negative		
I	wasn't (was not)	at home this morning.
You/We/They	weren't (were not)	
He/She/It	wasn't (was not)	

1 Complete the sentences with *was/were* (✔) or *wasn't/weren't* (✘).

It *wasn't* a very good film. (✘)

1 Gutenberg .... a printer, not a writer. (✔)

2 I .... at Adam's house after school. (✘)

3 The special effects in that film .... amazing. (✔)

4 You .... at home when I called. (✘)

5 We .... small children when they invented the Internet. (✔)

Past simple (regular and irregular verbs)

We use the **past simple** to talk about actions, events, situations or habits in the past. We form the past simple of regular verbs by adding ***-ed*** or ***-d*** to the verb. This is the same for all subjects.

2 Complete the sentences with the past simple form of the verbs in brackets.

I *liked* the documentary on TV last night. (**like**)

1 Kate .... at the end of the movie because it was so sad. (**cry**)

2 It's lucky that you .... the file on your computer. (**save**)

3 Long ago, people .... on cave walls. (**paint**)

4 We .... for new clothes yesterday. (**shop**)

5 Before the printing press, they .... books by hand. (**copy**)

Irregular verbs do NOT form the past simple by adding ***-ed.*** They have a different past form.

Present:	come	do	get	go	have	make	see
Past:	came	did	got	went	had	made	saw

3 Complete the sentences with the past simple form of the verbs in brackets.

I *bought* a new DVD yesterday. (**buy**)

1 Lewis .... a great website to help us with our project. (**find**)

2 Judy and Kate .... to the Halloween Fair. (**go**)

3 We .... all the old *Star Wars* movies on DVD. (**see**)

4 I .... you an email last night. Did you read it? (**send**)

5 Some people .... the printing press was a bad idea. (**think**)

The **negative** of the past simple is ***did not*** and the bare infinitive of the main verb. This is the same for regular and irregular verbs, and the same for all subjects. The short form is ***didn't***.

*I/You/He/She/We/They **didn't** watch TV last night.*

*I/You/He/She/We/They **didn't** think the film was exciting.*

Negative		
I/ You/We/They	didn't (did not) know	the answer.
He/She/It		

4 Write these sentences in the negative.

I wrote a letter to my grandmother.

I didn't write a letter to my grandmother.

1 People had books and emails twenty thousand years ago.

....

2 Columbus went to Australia.

....

3 Gutenberg invented the Internet.

....

4 Kate Winslet and Johnny Depp starred in *Jaws*.

....

5 Computers became popular before there was television.

....

Past simple question form (*was/were*)

We make questions with ***be*** in the past simple by putting ***was*** or ***were*** before the subject.

Was *it a good film?*

Were *you/we/they frightened?*

5 Write questions with the past simple of *be* and these words. Then write affirmative (✔) or negative (✘) short answers.

it / an exciting film? ✔

Was it an exciting film? Yes, it was.

1 the special effects / good? ✔

....

2 you and Kate / surprised by the ending? ✘

....

3 Lewis / at the cinema with you? ✘

....

4 Adam and Kate / frightened? ✔

....

5 the film / confusing? ✘

....

Past simple question form (*did*)

We make questions in the past simple by putting ***Did*** before the subject, and then the bare infinitive of the main verb. This is the same for regular and irregular verbs, and the same for all subjects.

Did *I/we/he/etc do something wrong?*

Did *you/he/she/they/etc enjoy the musical?*

In short answers, we use ***did*** or ***didn't***. We DON'T use the main verb.

6 Write questions from these sentences. Then write affirmative (✔) or negative (✘) short answers.

Gutenberg made the first printed book. ✔

Did Gutenberg make the first printed book? Yes, he did.

1 The Wright brothers flew the first aeroplane. ✔

....

2 We had television a hundred years ago. ✘

....

3 Leonardo DiCaprio wrote *Titanic*. ✘

....

4 Charlie Chaplin starred in lots of comedies. ✔

....

5 The Samarians invented the pyramids. ✘

....

We can use question words to ask for information. We begin with the question word, followed by ***was/were*** or ***did***.

What *was Spielberg's first film? – Firelight.*

What time *did the film start? – At 8 o'clock.*

Where *were you yesterday? – At home.*

Most question words begin with ***Wh-*** but we can also use ***How***, ***How much/many***, ***How long***, etc.

How *did they do the special effects? – They used computers.*

How much *money did the film make? – $1.8 billion.*

7 Write the questions for these answers.

They made the film in 2006.

When did they make the film?

1 The film was three hours long.

....

2 Johnny Depp starred as Captain Jack Sparrow.

....

3 The documentary was about animals.

....

4 Harry Potter went to school at Hogwarts.

....

-ing and *-ed* adjectives

When something makes a person feel excitement, surprise, interest, etc, we use ***-ing*** adjectives to describe the thing, and ***-ed*** adjectives to describe the person.

*The lesson was interest**ing**.*	*The students were interest**ed**.*
*The programme was bor**ing**.*	*I was bor**ed**.*

8 Choose the correct words to complete the conversation.

A: Did you like the film? I was a bit ~~*frightening*~~ / *frightened* at the end.

B: I wasn't. I thought it was really (1) *boring* / *bored* most of the time.

A: I'm (2) *amazing* / *amazed* you didn't like it. Don't you think the part with the snakes was (3) *exciting* / *excited*?

B: OK, that part was (4) *interesting* / *interested* but I couldn't understand what was happening. I was so (5) *confusing* / *confused*.

A: Maybe you were just (6) *tiring* / *tired* and that's why you didn't enjoy it.

4A Facing the lion

Vocabulary: life events

1 **Match the verbs (1–10) with the words (a–j). Some verbs match with more than one word.**

1 leave	**a** up
2 have	**b** to school
3 be	**c** a family
4 get	**d** from university
5 go	**e** married
6 grow	**f** an exam
7 graduate	**g** school
8 go	**h** job
9 pass	**i** born
10 get a	**j** to university

2 **Write the correct expression from Exercise 1 under each picture.**

a ....

b ....

c ....

d ....

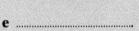

e ....

f ....

g ....

h ....

i ....

j ....

3 **Put the life events (a–j) from Exercise 2 in a logical order.**

1	**6** ....
2	**7** ....
3	**8** ....
4	**9** ....
5	**10** ....

4 **Complete the text with the verbs in the box.**

became	got married	graduated	grew up
left	met	passed	travelled	~~was~~	went

My grandmother *was* born in 1952 in north-east Australia. She [1] .... on a farm in the outback, where she lived with her parents and her brother. She [2] .... to school every day by bus, to the next town. Many of the students were Aboriginal people. She worked hard and [3] .... all her exams. When she [4] .... school, she [5] .... to university in Sydney, where she studied medicine. She [6] .... from university in 1975, and [7] .... a doctor in a big hospital. She [8] .... my grandfather in a restaurant in 1977 and they [9] .... in 1979.

Grammar: past continuous

5 Complete the text with the correct past continuous form of the verbs in brackets.

Last Saturday evening, I [1] .... (do) my homework at the kitchen table. I [2] .... (study) maths for an exam on Monday. My parents [3] .... (sit) at the kitchen table, too. They [4] .... (play) cards. They [5] .... (not talk) loudly, but it was difficult to concentrate, so I decided to go and study in my room. My brother [6] .... (play) computer games in his room with his friends. They [7] .... (make) a lot of noise so I asked them to go and watch TV in the living room. Ten minutes later, I heard loud music and people shouting. It [8] .... (come) from outside. The neighbours [9] .... (have) a party!

6 Complete the story with the past continuous form of the verbs in the box.

carry	look	play	not eat	sit
talk	wait			

Last Sunday, the weather was hot and sunny so we went for a picnic in the park. We found a big tree and sat under it. Everything was perfect. The boys [1] .... football and the girls [2] .... on the grass in the shade. The food was in a big basket under the tree. I [3] .... to my friends. We were very hungry, but we [4] .... the picnic food. We [5] .... for the boys to finish their game. Suddenly, I saw something on the food basket. I went to investigate. It was a huge ant and it [6] .... at me! I opened the basket quickly and screamed. There were enormous ants everywhere! They [7] .... food from the basket to the tree. The picnic was ruined! We threw the food in the bin and went home.

7 Read the story in Exercise 6 again. Write *Wh*- questions with the past continuous form of the verbs. Then answer the questions.

What / boys / play / ?

What were the boys playing?
They were playing football.

1 Where / girls / sit?

....

....

2 What / girls / do?

....

....

3 Who / you / talk to?

....

....

4 What / ants / carry?

....

....

Working with words: time expressions

8 Choose the correct option (a, b or c) to complete the text.

Last Saturday night, we went camping near a river. We put up our tents and made a fire. We had some supper and [1] .... we went to bed. [2] .... we got into our tents, the sky was clear but it was a bit windy. We were all very tired and fell asleep quickly. But, [3] .... the night, there was a terrible storm. We looked outside and saw lots of lightning. [4] ...., we heard a loud crash and saw a big tree fall to the ground. [5] ...., we were quite frightened but we finally went back to sleep. Two hours [6] ...., the wind blew the tent away and we woke up with no tent!

1 a suddenly **b** when **c** then
2 a During **b** When **c** Then
3 a later **b** then **c** during
4 a Suddenly **b** When **c** During
5 a Later **b** After that **c** Suddenly
6 a after **b** ago **c** later

4B Wanted, dead or alive!

Grammar: past simple and past continuous

1 Complete the sentences with the past simple or the past continuous form of the verb in brackets.

1 While my grandmother .... (study) to be a doctor, she also .... (work) as a waitress in a restaurant in Sydney.

2 One day, she .... (work) in the restaurant when three doctors from the hospital .... (come) in and asked for a table.

3 While they .... (order) their meal, one of the doctors said that he .... (celebrate) his birthday. It was my grandfather and it was his twenty-ninth birthday.

4 My grandfather often saw my grandmother at the hospital and he was in love with her. That day, in the restaurant, he .... (watch) her all the time while she .... (serve) the customers.

5 At the end of the meal, my grandmother came to their table. While she .... (take) their order for coffee, he .... (put) a note in her pocket.

6 While the men .... (have) coffee, my grandmother .... (read) the note. It said:

Hi. How about dinner tomorrow?
Ralph
P.S. I'm the new doctor in Accident and Emergency

7 Then the boss asked my grandmother to help in the kitchen for a while. When she .... (come) back into the restaurant, the three doctors .... (leave).

8 When my grandfather .... (look) back into the restaurant, my grandmother .... (write) 'YES' on the window!

Vocabulary: appearance

2 Look at the pictures and write at least three words or phrases to describe each man.

1 *slim,* .... , ...
2 *beard,* .... , ...
3 *long hair,* .... , ...

3 4.1 Listen to the news report about a robbery. Which picture in Exercise 2 doesn't match any of the descriptions?

Picture ....

4 Read the news report. Look at the artist's drawing of the third robber below. Rewrite the description with the correct information.

Third Man in High Street Robbery?

This morning, a witness gave the police more information about the robbery in the High Street last Wednesday. He was taking rubbish to his bin when he noticed a black Volkswagen Golf parked outside his house. 'I could see the driver very clearly because there was a street lamp next to the car,' he said. Here is an artist's drawing of the driver.

'She was quite an old woman, probably in her fifties. She was short and fat and had short, dark hair. She was wearing a white T-shirt and had a tattoo on her neck. She wasn't wearing make-up. She was also wearing a nose-ring.'

If you know who this woman is, please contact Otterton police station.

Johnny Depp in *Pirates of the Caribbean*

5 Look at this photo of Johnny Depp as Jack Sparrow. Complete the description with the words in the box.

moustache black dark (x2) beard beads tattoos scar

In the film, *Pirates of the Caribbean*, Johnny Depp had long, [1] b.............................. hair and very [2] d.............................. eyes. He had really [3] d.............................. skin and a black [4] b............................... He also had a [5] m.............................. He didn't have a [6] s.............................. on his face but he had lots of [7] t.............................. on his arms. He also wore a leather pirate's hat called a tricorne and wore [8] b.............................. and coins in his hair.

Reading

6 Look at the pictures and complete the words. (You can find all the words in the text on the right.)

1 a sw................. **2** a sc................. **3** a t.................

4 an is................. **5** a sai................. s.................

7 Read the text. Choose the best heading (a–d) for each paragraph (1–4).

a A lost bag
b Jack Sparrow's childhood
c The magic powers of the Sword of Cortés
d Jack leaves home

The young Jack Sparrow

Most people know who Captain Jack Sparrow is. He is the handsome pirate in the *Pirates of the Caribbean* films. He is played by Johnny Depp. He is clever, funny and dangerous. But who exactly was Jack Sparrow?

1 ....

Jack Sparrow was born on a ship during a bad storm. His father was a pirate captain. We don't really know what happened to his mother, but she probably died when Jack was a baby. Jack grew up in Shipwreck Cove, where he lived with his grandmother. His father spent his time at sea, so Jack didn't see him very often.

2 ....

Jack's grandmother was often horrible to Jack. When he was about 16 years old, Jack decided to leave home and to look for adventure. He put a few things in a bag and ran away. He hid on a ship and, many weeks later, he arrived on Tortuga. This small Caribbean island was where pirates sometimes stayed, including the violent and dangerous Captain Torrents. Tortuga was not a safe place for a young boy to be.

3 ....

One day, while he wasn't looking, somebody stole Jack's bag. He saw it a few days later. It was in the tavern, under Captain Torrents' chair. While Captain Torrents was talking and drinking, Jack took the bag and escaped from the tavern. Later, when he looked inside the bag, he discovered that the bag wasn't his. It was Captain's Torrents'! Inside the bag, he found the scabbard of the Sword of Cortés.

4 ....

Later, Jack learned that the scabbard gave the Sword of Cortés magic powers. This gave Jack the idea for his first real adventure. He found an old sailing ship called the *Barnacle* and, together with his friend Arabella and a young boy called Fitwilliam, he set off to find the Sword of Cortés. While they were sailing on the Caribbean seas, they had lots of adventures and also fought with Captain Torrents many times. Jack eventually found the Sword of Cortés.

8 Read the text again and answer the questions.

Where was Jack born? *He was born on a pirate ship.*

1 What did he do when he was sixteen?

....

2 What wasn't Jack doing when somebody stole his bag?

....

3 When did Jack take his bag and escape?

....

4 What did he find in Captain Torrents' bag?

....

5 What were Jack and his friends looking for?

....

6 What happened while they were sailing the Caribbean?

....

4C Apologising

1 Look at the pictures. Use the words in the box to write the dialogues.

a

very	I'm	sorry	It	matter	doesn't

Boy: ....!
Girl: ....

b

Never	right	It's	all	mind

Mum: ....!
Dad: .... I can fix it.

2 Now use the expressions from Exercise 1 to complete the dialogue.

Simon: Hi, Claire. Did you bring my book?
Claire: I'm [1] .... I left it at home.
Simon: Never [2] .... Did you finish reading it?
Claire: Not yet. Do you want it back soon?
Simon: It's [3] .... You can keep it until you finish it.
Claire: Thanks, Simon.

3 Complete the dialogues. Choose the correct option (a or b).

a Paul and Declan are talking on the phone.

1 (a) say (b) apologise
2 (a) forgot (b) was forgetting
3 (a) matter (b) mind
4 (a) right (b) good

Declan: Hi, Paul. I want to [1] .... sorry. I [2] .... to send you a birthday card.
Paul: Never [3] .... It happens every year.
Declan: It's just that I was visiting family over the Christmas holidays.
Paul: It's all [4] .... People are always busy on 26 December. It's a really bad day for a birthday!

b Joshua is talking to Sarah at lunchtime.

1 (a) sorry (b) bad
2 (a) matter (b) mind
3 (a) was having (b) had
4 (a) worry (b) mind

Joshua: Sarah. I'm really [1] .... I can't find your highlighter pen.
Sarah: Oh, it doesn't [2] .... I've got lots more.
Joshua: I [3] .... it in my bag this morning and now it isn't there!
Sarah: Don't [4] .... about it. It's only a pen!

4 Use the words to write two apologising dialogues.

a

Sarah: sorry / lose / earrings
Claire: not worry / OK
Sarah: think / left / at party
Claire: not matter / old / never wear

b

Joshua: sorry / break / CD
Paul: never mind / not matter
Joshua: break / take out of / box
Paul: not worry / not like group anymore / never listen

Pronunciation: /æ/, /e/ and /ɜː/

5 4.2 Listen and circle the word you hear.

1 bad bed
2 bird bad
3 head heard
4 lend learned
5 man men
6 first fast
7 ten turn
8 hat hurt

Writing: a biography

6 Read the biography of Johnny Depp. Complete the text with the words in the box.

later when (x2) after (x2) while

My favourite actor – Johnny Depp

Johnny Depp is famous for his roles in many different films. He is probably most famous for his role as Jack Sparrow in *Pirates of the Caribbean.*

John Christopher Depp was born on 9 June, 1963 in Kentucky, in the USA. He grew up in Florida. His mother bought him a guitar [1] .... he was twelve and his ambition was to be a rock musician. He left school [2] .... he was seventeen and became a musician in different bands.

[3] .... he became an actor. In 1984, he got a small part in *A Nightmare on Elm Street*. In 1990, the director Tim Burton gave him the role of Edward Scissorhands. [4] .... that, he was in lots of films, including *Pirates of the Caribbean: The Curse of the Black Pearl* (2003), *Finding Neverland* (2004) and *Sweeny Todd* (2007). He was nominated for an Oscar for his roles in these films, but he didn't win.

[5] .... he finished filming *The Curse of the Black Pearl*, Johnny Depp decided to keep his beard and moustache and he grew his hair long. He's also got 13 tattoos, just like a pirate! He often wears glasses.

Johnny Depp's first famous girlfriend was the actress Sherilyn Fenn. He also *dated* Winona Ryder, who was his co-star in *Edward Scissorhands*, and had a three-year relationship with the model Kate Moss. In 1998, Johnny Depp met the French pop singer Vanessa Paradis [6] .... he was filming in Paris. They had a daughter, Lily-Rose Melody, in 1999 and a son, Jack, in 2002. They are still together.

dated = go out with, have a relationship with

7 Read the biography again and complete the notes.

Date of birth: 9th June, 1963
1 Nationality: ....
2 Appearance: ....
3 Ambition when young: ....
4 First important film role: ....
5 Most famous role: ....
6 Girlfriends: ....
7 Family: ....

8 Use the notes below to complete the biography of Marie Curie. Remember to use linking words like *then, when* and *after.*

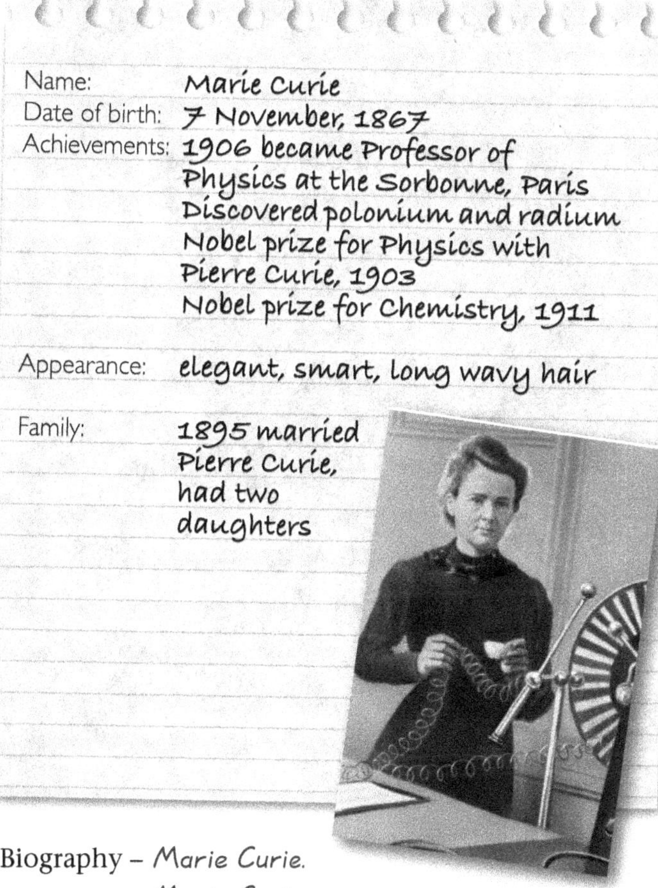
Name: Marie Curie
Date of birth: 7 November, 1867
Achievements: 1906 became Professor of Physics at the Sorbonne, Paris
Discovered polonium and radium
Nobel prize for Physics with Pierre Curie, 1903
Nobel prize for Chemistry, 1911
Appearance: elegant, smart, long wavy hair
Family: 1895 married Pierre Curie, had two daughters

Biography – *Marie Curie.*
Marie Curie was a scientist.
She was born on ...

9 Now write a biography about a famous person you admire. First write notes, then write the text.

4D Explore more

Hi Emily,

It was great to see you last Saturday. I really enjoyed the concert. We've got a day's holiday on Friday. Do you want to do something? There's a music festival in the park in the afternoon and I've got two free tickets. Phone me if you want to come.

Claire

1 Read the email from Claire. Choose the correct option (a, b, c or d).

Claire wrote to Emily to:

a thank Emily for the concert
b talk about Saturday
c invite Emily
d give Emily her opinion about the concert

2 Read Claire's email again. Underline the words that helped you answer question 1.

3 Read the note and choose the correct option (a, b or c).

Hi Sarah,
I didn't find your pen so I bought some new ones this morning. While I was paying for them, I saw this really cool notebook so I bought it for you.
I hope you like it.
Joshua

Joshua wrote the note to:

a ask Sarah to go shopping
b offer Sarah the notebook
c talk about his morning

4 Read the email and choose the correct option (a, b or c).

Dear Aunty Magda,

I really enjoyed Christmas at your house and I loved being with my cousins. Dan and I became great friends. Why don't you all come to our house at Easter? Mum says we can sleep on the floor!

Love,

Declan

Declan wrote the email to:

a say thank you
b make a suggestion
c tell his aunt about Christmas

Listening

5 4.3 Listen to the question and choose the best response (a, b or c). You can listen twice.

a It was raining at the beach.
b We went to the beach.
c Let's go to the beach.

6 4.4 Listen to the statement and choose the best response (a, b or c). You can listen twice.

a I agree!
b I'm really sorry.
c What's the matter?

7 4.5 Listen to four statements twice. Choose the best response (a, b or c).

1 a I don't agree.
b OK. We can go tomorrow.
c Don't worry. It doesn't matter.

2 a We went to the cinema.
b Let's go to the cinema.
c I prefer the cinema.

3 a Don't worry. It's all right.
b I read it yesterday.
c No, I haven't. It's at home.

4 a It isn't on my desk.
b I'm sorry. I forgot to do it.
c Don't worry. It's all right.

Word list Unit 4

achievement (n) ....
amount (n) ....
ancestor (n) ....
ancient (adj) ....
apologise (v) ....
appearance (n) ....
armour (n) ....
bang (v) ....
battle (n) ....
bead (n) ....
beard (n) ....
bird (n) ....
blow away (phr v) ....
bracelet (n) ....
career (n) ....
cell (n) ....
chase (v) ....
childhood (n) ....
coin (n) ....
contestant (n) ....
cow (n) ....
crash (n) ....
curly (adj) ....
cut off (phr v) ....
curling irons (n pl) ....
dead (adj) ....
death (n) ....
desert (n) ....
disappear (v) ....
escape (v) ....
exist (v) ....
expedition (n) ....
face (n) ....
fall (v) ....
fall asleep (phr v) ....
famous (adj) ....
fashionable (adj) ....
fear (n) ....
forget (v) ....
frequent (adj) ....
government (n) ....
graduate (v) ....
grow up (phr v) ....
glands (n pl) ....
heat (n) ....

hairstyle (n) ....
handsome (adj) ....
hero (n) ....
heroic (adj) ....
hit (v) ....
hungry (adj) ....
important (adj) ....
investigate (v) ....
invite (v) ....
it doesn't matter (phr) ....
jump (v) ....
kill (v) ....
later (adv) ....
lay (past simple) (v) ....
leather (adj) ....
lightning (n) ....
loud (adj) ....
male (adj) ....
midnight (n) ....
mountain (n) ....
moustache (n) ....
neighbour (n) ....
never mind (phr) ....
noise (n) ....
nomad (n) ....
once more (phr) ....
outback (n) ....
painter (n) ....
painting (n) ....
pass an exam (phr) ....
prison (n) ....
powder (n) ....
reach (v) ....
relationship (n) ....
remember (v) ....
repeatedly (adv) ....
return (v) ....
roar (n) ....
rod (n) ....
robbery (n) ....
root (n) ....
Royal Navy (n) ....
rubbish (n) ....
sebum (n) ....
scabbard (n) ....

shade (n) ....
shaft (n) ....
shake (v) ....
share (v) ....
shark (n) ....
shoot (v) ....
short (adj) ....
snore (v) ....
spirit (n) ....
spiky (adj) ....
strange (adj) ....
strand (n) ....
surrender (v) ....
trap (n) ....
tail (n) ....
the Middle Ages (phr) ....
tricorne (n) ....
trendy (adj) ....
wavy (adj) ....
while (adv) ....
witness (n) ....
worry (v) ....
young (adj) ....

U4 Reading Explorer

ancestor (n) ....
bang (v) ....
cell (n) ....
curling irons (n pl) ....
glands (n pl) ....
hairstyle (n) ....
heat (n) ....
powder (n) ....
rod (n) ....
root (n) ....
sebum (n) ....
shaft (n) ....
spiky (adj) ....
strand (n) ....
the Middle Ages (phr) ....
trap (n) ....
trendy (adj) ....

Past continuous

We use **past continuous** to talk about actions that were happening at a particular time in the past.

*I **was studying** at eight o'clock yesterday evening.*

We form the past continuous with ***was/were*** and the main verb with ***-ing***.

*The dog **was sitting** on the sofa a minute ago.*

*We **were lying** on the beach at this time yesterday.*

With verbs ending in a **consonant** + ***-e***, we change the ***-e*** to ***-ing***.

close closing take taking

With most verbs ending in a **single vowel** + **a consonant**, we double the consonant and add ***-ing***.

stop stopping put putting

With verbs ending in ***-ie***, we change the ***-ie*** to ***-ying***.

lie lying die dying

We form the negative with ***wasn't/weren't***.

*I **wasn't** trying to be funny, but everyone laughed.*

*I showed you, but you **weren't** watching!*

1 Complete the sentences with *was/were* (✔) or *wasn't/weren't* (✘).

It *was* raining hard this morning. (✔)

1 He crashed because he .... driving carefully. (✘)
2 I .... playing football at this time yesterday. (✔)
3 We .... waiting for you after school. Where were you? (✔)
4 The girls .... watching TV last night. (✘)
5 You .... making a lot of noise in class today. (✔)
6 I .... talking about you when I said that. (✘)

2 Complete the sentences with the *-ing* form of the verbs in brackets.

Where's Angela? She was *sitting* here a minute ago. (**sit**)

1 The ship was .... gold and silver to England. (**take**)
2 They were .... the house when I got there. (**leave**)
3 I was .... on the sofa when you called. (**lie**)
4 We were .... our books on the shelf when it fell down. (**put**)
5 Dad was .... around Spain when he met Mum. (**travel**)
6 Joseph was .... with fear when he saw the lion. (**shake**)

3 Complete the sentences with the past continuous form of the verbs in brackets.

I *was reading* (read) an interesting book this afternoon.

1 The students .... (not write) a history test at ten o'clock.
2 You .... (ask) a lot of questions in the lesson.
3 Lynne didn't hear what the teacher said because she .... (not listen).
4 We .... (send) each other text messages all evening.
5 Why did you move? I .... (take) a photo of you!

4 *What was happening at 8:30 yesterday evening?* Write negative (✘) and affirmative (✔) sentences in the past continuous with these words.

My parents / watch / TV ✘ They / have dinner ✔

My parents weren't watching TV. They were having dinner.

1 I / do / my homework ✘ I / practise / the guitar ✔

....

2 You / study ✘ You / listen to music ✔

....

3 We / think / about school ✘ We / have / fun ✔

....

4 Maria / cook / dinner ✘ She / wait / for a friend ✔

....

5 Barry / sleep ✘ He / talk / to Sarah on the phone ✔

....

6 Adam and Lewis / read ✘ They / play / computer games ✔

....

We make questions in past continuous by putting ***Was/Were*** before the subject, and then the main verb with ***-ing***.

***Was** the sun shining this morning?*

***Were** you watching the nine o'clock news on TV?*

In short answers we use ***was/wasn't*** or ***were/weren't***. We don't use the main verb.

5 Write questions in the past continuous with these words.

you and Kate / talk / on the phone last night?

Were you and Kate talking on the phone last night?

1 Lewis / wait / for you at the cinema?

....

2 I / make / a lot of noise?

....

3 you / try / to call me five minutes ago?

....

4 the boys / play / football in the classroom?

....

5 it / rain / at lunchtime?

....

6 Now write affirmative (✔) or negative (✘) short answers to the questions in Exercise 5.

(Were you and Kate talking on the phone last night?) (✔) *Yes, we were.*

1 (✘) ....
2 (✔) ....
3 (✔) ....
4 (✘) ....
5 (✔) ....

7 Put the words into the correct order to make questions.

watching / you / this afternoon / were / the carnival / ?

Were you watching the carnival this afternoon?

1 the people next door / a party / last night / having / were / ?

....

2 was / to our conversation / your brother / listening / ?

....

3 Adam / trying / something / to tell us / was / ?

....

4 very loudly / were / talking / we / ?

....

We can use question words to ask for information. We begin with the question word, followed by ***was/were.***

***What** were you doing at nine o'clock last night? – Phoning a friend.*

***Who** were you phoning? – Judy.*

***Why** were you phoning her? – To ask about our homework.*

***Where** were you phoning from? – From my bedroom.*

8 Write the questions for these answers.

I was watching an adventure film yesterday evening.

What were you watching yesterday evening?

1 We were talking to Lewis earlier.

....

2 Judy was going to Kate's house when I saw her.

....

3 They were hurrying this morning because they were late.

....

4 Dad was buying a present for Mum at lunchtime.

....

Past simple and past continuous

We use **past continuous** for an action that was already happening at the time when a second action happened or began; we use **past simple** for the second action.

***I was moving** the computer to my bedroom* (past continuous) *when I **dropped** it.* (past simple)

We use ***when*** **+ past simple** OR ***while*** **+ past continuous** to talk about the two actions together.

I was having a bath (past continuous) ***when** the phone **rang**.* (**past simple**)

The phone rang (past simple) **while** *I **was having** a bath.* (**past continuous**)

We can put the two actions in any order, but we must still use ***when*** **+ past simple** OR ***while*** **+ past continuous.**

***When** the phone **rang**,* (**past simple**) *I was having a bath.* (past continuous)

***While** I **was having** a bath,* (**past continuous**) *the phone rang.* (past simple)

9 Complete the sentences with *when* or *while.*

I was watching TV *when* you called.

1 .... I was doing my homework, the computer crashed.
2 I heard a noise in the living room .... I was studying.
3 .... I arrived at the station, the train was leaving.
4 He was driving very fast .... the accident happened.
5 They told me the news .... I was having breakfast.

10 Complete the sentences with the past simple or past continuous form of the verbs in brackets.

While I *was using* (use) your pen, it *broke* (break).

1 Someone .... (steal) her purse while she .... (not look).
2 We .... (have) a picnic when it .... (start) raining.
3 When the lesson .... (begin) he .... (finish) his homework.
4 I .... (take) some photos while they .... (dance).
5 While you .... (sleep), I .... (borrow) your MP3 player.

Review Units 3 and 4

1 Circle the correct auxiliary verb.

(Can) / do he sing well ?

1 *Have / Has* you got a bike?
2 *Can / Is* you play the piano?
3 *Are / Do* they live in Italy?
4 *Does / Is* Jenny listening to music?
5 *Do / Are* the children playing in the garden?
6 *Did / Are* we going to the cinema tonight?
7 *Can / Do* you help me, please?
8 *Was / Did* it sunny yesterday?
9 *Did / Have* you enjoy the concert?
10 *Was / Did* he singing in the shower?

1 mark per item: ... / 10 marks

2 Make these sentences into questions. Don't forget the question mark.

You bought a new mobile phone last week.
Did you buy a new mobile phone last week?

1 He's got a cat.
2 They can play the piano.
3 They're from Mexico.
4 Her cousins live in London.
5 Simon is studying in the library.
6 You like playing tennis.
7 He was in the school play.
8 They watched TV last night.
9 The cat ran up a tree.
10 You were having breakfast when I phoned.

1 mark per item: ... / 10 marks

3 Complete the questions and write *Yes / No* answers.

1 .... you studying English now?
....
2 .... the teacher got a CD player?
....
3 .... it foggy this morning?
....
4 .... your family watch TV last night?
....
5 .... the chess club start at four o'clock?
....
6 .... you washing your hair when I phoned last night?
....
7 I don't understand the maths homework. .... you help me?
....

2 marks per item: ... / 14 marks

4 Write questions for the answers.

1 Where / Mike? ....
He's in the playground.
2 What / doing? ....
He's talking to a girl.
3 Who / she? ....
His friend, Alison.
4 Why / she / crying? ....
She broke her watch.
5 When / it / happen? ....
About ten minutes ago.
6 How much / it / cost? ....
About £40.
7 Where / go / last night? ....
I went to the cinema.
8 Who / go / with? ....
My brother and his friend.
9 What / see? ....
The new James Bond film.
10 What time / get / home?
....
About nine o'clock, I think.

1 mark per item: ... / 10 marks

5 Choose the correct option.

1 My family bought a big, new TV four days *ago / later.*
2 *When / Then* we got home, we decided to watch a DVD.
3 We were enjoying the film *when / while* the phone rang. My mum answered it, but there was no-one there.
4 Five minutes *ago / later*, the phone rang again.
5 *When / After that* Mum answered, she heard a laugh.
6 *After that / Later*, we turned the phone off and watched the rest of the film.

1 mark per item: ... / 6 marks

6 Read the definitions and write the words.

1 It was a very frightening film. The special effects were very real!

h.............................. f..............................

2 We saw it at the cinema. It was very funny.

c..............................

3 It's about people living in the same street and it started thirty years ago!

s.............................. o..............................

4 The guests are very interesting and the presenter asks good questions.

c.............................. s..............................

5 This week, a contestant answered all the questions correctly and won a million pounds!

q.............................. s..............................

6 It's set in France in the 17th century. There are lots of famous actors in it.

d..............................

7 It's very small and I listen to it when I go running. I put my favourite songs on it.

i..............................

8 I write it at the weekend and my friends can read it on *Facebook*.

b..............................

9 My dad listens to it on the radio in the morning. I like the bit about the sport.

n..............................

10 My mum watches lots of these. She loves the ones about wild animals.

d..............................

2 marks per item: ... / 20 marks

7 Put the life events in a logical order.

1 leave school, be born, go to school

....

2 get a job, go to university, graduate

....

3 get a job, leave school, have a family

....

4 leave home, grow up, get married

....

5 have a family, leave home, get married

....

2 marks per item: ... / 10 marks

8 Complete the description. Choose the correct option.

The girl has got 1 *straight / wavy*, black hair. She's got 2 *dark / fair* skin and blue eyes. She's got 3 *tattoos / scars* on her arms. She isn't wearing 4 *a nose-ring / make-up*. Her boyfriend is 5 *tall / short* and 6 *slim / fat*. He's got 7 *short / long*, 8 *fair / dark* hair and a small 9 *moustache / beard*. He's wearing a(n) 10 *earring / nose-ring*.

1 mark per item: ... / 10 marks

9 Write adjectives with *-ed* or *-ing*.

1 The children were .... by the storm. (frighten)

2 The film was terrible. I was really .... (bore)

3 We're going to Paris tomorrow. We're really .... (excite)

4 We went for a long walk in the mountains. It was very .... (tire)

5 The ending of the film was strange. I was .... (confuse)

6 When I phoned my friend in Australia, she was very .... (surprise)

1 mark per item: ... / 6 marks

10 Match the statements (1–4) with the responses (a–d).

1 What do you think, Sam?

2 I love romantic comedies!

3 I'm sorry. I left your DVD at home.

4 Johnny Depp is a brilliant actor.

a I don't agree. He's OK, but he's not fantastic.

b Never mind. You can give it to me tomorrow.

c I agree with Paul.

d Me too! My favourite is *You've Got Mail*.

1 mark per item: ... / 4 marks

Total marks: ... / 100

5A Extreme animals

Vocabulary: animals

1 Label the pictures of wild animals.

1 a ....
2 a ....
3 a ....
4 a ....
5 a ....
6 an ....
7 a ....
8 a ....
9 a ....
10 a ....
11 a ....
12 an ....
13 a ....
14 an ....

2 Complete the sentences with the adjectives in the box.

friendly ugly ~~long~~ heavy intelligent poisonous small dangerous ~~tall~~

Giraffes have *long* necks and eat the leaves from *tall* trees.

1 Some snakes are .... They can kill you.
2 Dogs love being with people – they are very .... animals.
3 Be careful of crocodiles. They can be ....!
4 You can train whales to perform in shows – they are very ....
5 Many people think snakes are ...., but I think they're beautiful.
6 Elephants are very .... animals. They weigh many kilos.
7 Mice are .... and furry. Some people keep them as pets.

Grammar: comparative adjectives

3 Write sentences with the comparative form + *than*.

Giraffes are *taller than* zebras. (tall)

1 Pigs are .... dogs. (intelligent)
2 Hippos are .... bears. (heavy)
3 A mouse is .... an ant. (big)
4 Dogs are .... cats. (friendly)
5 Rabbits are .... pets .... hamsters. (good)
6 Lions are .... horses. (dangerous)
7 Ants are .... tortoises. (active)

4 Write the adjectives and their comparative forms in the correct column of the table.

1 syllable	ending in 'y'	2+ syllables	irregular
longer	....	....	....
....	....	....	....
....	....	....	....
....	....	....	....
....	....	....	....

~~long~~ dangerous heavy quick slow active good small ugly intelligent big friendly poisonous bad

Comparative adjectives: questions

5 Write questions for the answers.

Which is more beautiful – a lion or a zebra?
I think a zebra is more beautiful than a lion.

1 ....?
I think maths is more important than art.

2 ....?
I think dogs are friendlier than cats.

3 ....?
I think Greece is hotter than Italy.

4 ....?
I think a lion is faster than an antelope.

5 ....?
I think snakes are more dangerous than crocodiles.

6 Write comparative sentences and questions.

biology / easy / physics.
Biology is easier than physics.

1 the Amazon / wide / the Danube.
....

2 whales / large / sharks.
....

3 my French / bad / my English.
....

4 London / big / expensive / Madrid.
....

5 a bear / strong / a horse?
....

6 hamsters / interesting / cats.
....

7 zoo animals / happy/ wild animals?
....

Working with words: *too* and *enough*

7 Write two sentences for each statement. Use *too* and *enough*.

I missed the bus. (slow / fast)
I was too slow.
I wasn't fast enough.

1 We didn't watch the horror film to the end. (scared / brave)
We ....
We ....

2 I didn't buy the trousers. (small / big)
They ....
They ....

3 Nobody is swimming in the sea today. (cold / hot)
It ....
It ....

4 I didn't finish the exam. (difficult / easy)
It ....
It ....

5 My brother didn't join the police. (short / tall)
He ....
He ....

8 Complete the text with the correct form of the adjectives in brackets. Add words where necessary.

Last Saturday, my little sister, Lily, said she wanted to go to the zoo. I don't really like the zoo – I prefer the safari park – but I went anyway. It was *better than* (good) staying at home on my own. First, we visited the monkey house and the lion house. I thought the monkeys and gorillas were [1] .... (interesting) the big cats. The lions didn't do anything! Lily said they were [2] .... (tired) to move!

In the afternoon, the sun came out so we had lunch outside. After that, we went to see the brown bears, but they didn't come out of their houses. Perhaps it was [3] .... (hot) for them.

I was surprised by the sharks. They were [4] .... (friendly) many other animals. They liked looking at the people through the glass. My favourite animals were the penguins. I think they were [5] .... (happy) the other zoo animals.

I actually enjoyed seeing the animals, but I still don't like zoos. I think animals are [6] .... (healthy) and lead [7] .... (natural) lives in safari parks.

5B Extreme Earth

Vocabulary: habitats

1 Write the missing letters in the puzzle to make 7 habitats.

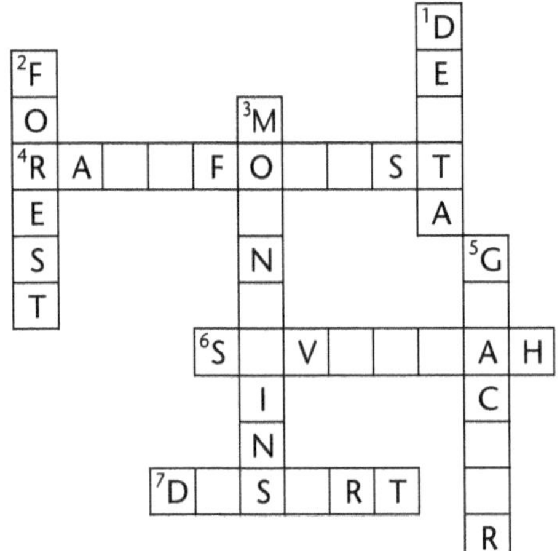

2 Match the definitions (1–6) with the words (a–f).

1 a large pool of water in the middle of land — d
2 living rock under the sea
3 It goes to the sea.
4 There is a famous one in Niagara.
5 flat land between two mountains or hills
6 a piece of land with water on all sides

a valley
b island
c coral reef
d lake
e river
f waterfall

Reading

3 Look at the photo and the map and answer the questions.

1 How did the men travel?
2 How many countries did they visit? Which countries were they? Write a list.

4 Read the text and check your answers to Exercise 3.

Long Way Round

Ewan McGregor was having a meal with his best friend Charley Boorman when they decided to ride round the world on their motorbikes. Ewan McGregor is one of Britain's most famous actors and Boorman is the son of the film director, John Boorman, but they are also ***mad about*** motorbikes.

Long Way Round is the film documentary of their adventure. They left London on 14 April, 2004 and rode east across nine countries, including France, Belgium, Germany, the Czech Republic, Slovakia, Ukraine, Russia, Kazakhstan, and Mongolia.

In Europe, they saw mountains and forests, green valleys and lakes. While travelling in Siberia, Kazakhstan and Mongolia they rode across some of the most isolated and beautiful ***landscapes*** in the world, including the Gobi Desert. It was also the most difficult and dangerous part of the world they travelled through. In Siberia, some rivers were too dangerous to cross and they had to put the bikes on trucks. While they were driving on a deserted road in Kazakhstan, a man in a passing car pointed a ***gun*** at them.

So, how did they film the journey? Ewan and Charley had cameras in their helmets and a cameraman followed with the ***crew***, who travelled in trucks. Ewan and Charley were faster on their bikes and the crew always arrived at their destinations a day or two later.

From Siberia, they flew to Alaska, then rode their bikes through Canada and the USA. They had many accidents on the trip but the worst one happened in the USA, when Ewan was ***hit*** by another bike. They finally arrived in New York on 29 July, 2004.

5 Read the text again. Are the sentences true or false?

	T	F
Ewan McGregor is Charley Boorman's best friend.	✔	☐
1 Ewan McGregor's father is a famous film director.	☐	☐
2 They travelled from London by train.	☐	☐
3 Travelling through Europe was easier than riding across Mongolia.	☐	☐
4 Some rivers were not safe enough to ride across.	☐	☐
5 Ewan and Charley often arrived at the next destination earlier than the crew.	☐	☐
6 The worst accident happened as they arrived in New York.	☐	☐

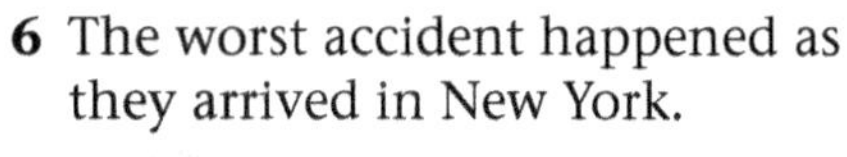

Tip!
Underline the sentences in the text which give you the answers to the questions.

Study skills: learning new words

6 Find the words and expressions *in italics* in the text and guess their meanings. Check in a dictionary.

'mad about' *to really like / be interested in*

Grammar: superlative adjectives

7 Complete the table with forms of the adjectives from the text.

Adjective	Comparative	Superlative
famous	....	....
....	....	the most beautiful
....	better	....
....	more difficult	....
....	more isolated	....
....	....	the worst
dangerous	....	....
fast	....	....

8 Complete the sentences with superlative adjectives from the table in Exercise 7.

1 Ewan McGregor is one of .... actors in the world. (famous)
2 Siberia is one of .... parts of the world to visit. (difficult)
3 Mongolia is one of .... regions in Asia. (isolated)
4 I think *Long Way Round* is .... DVD documentary you can buy. (good)
5 Europe has got .... mountains and lakes in the world. (beautiful)
6 The Gobi Desert is one of .... habitats in the world. (dry)

9 Complete the sentences with the comparative or superlative form of the adjectives in brackets.

Adventure holidays

Caving, diving or trekking? Which adventure holiday is the [1] .... (exciting)? Which holiday is the [2] .... (good) for you? When you go caving, you go underground into [3] .... (big) caves in the world. But caving is [4] .... (wet) and [5] .... (cold) than trekking. Trekking in the desert is [6] .... (hot) activity you can do. Diving in the Pacific is probably [7] .... (dangerous) than caving or trekking. The Pacific has [8] .... (large) sharks and [9] .... (poisonous) fish in the world!

Grammar: *have to*

10 Make true sentences or questions with the correct form of *have to*.

bikers / wear helmets.
Bikers have to wear helmets.

1 you / go from Siberia to Alaska by plane.
....
2 students / go to school on Sundays.
....
3 people who go trekking / wear socks.
....
4 base jumpers / do special training?
....
5 farmers / get up early?
....

Listening

11 Label the pictures.

rafting | sea canoeing | cycling | river swimming

a 
....

b 
....

c 
....

d 
....

12 5.1 **Listen to Jenny talking about her holiday. Tick (✓) the best picture (a–d) in Exercise 11.**

13 Listen again and choose the correct option.

Jenny went on holiday with
her sister / *her best friend.*

1 They went to a small country *in the mountains* / *by the sea.*
2 They did a lot of *climbing* / *walking.*
3 They didn't swim in the river. It wasn't *safe enough* / *warm enough.*
4 Hal didn't go rafting. He was too *young* / *scared.*
5 Jenny is *worse* / *better* than Hal at swimming.
6 Hal was good at *motor sports* / *canoeing.*

5C Shopping

Vocabulary: clothes

1 Emma is buying a sweatshirt. Complete the dialogue with the expressions in the box. There is one extra expression.

Yes, but we've only got it in black. Can I help you?
How is it? Is it big enough? It's £27.99.
Sweatshirts are over there.
Yes, of course. This is a small, is that your size?

Assistant: 1 ....
Emma: Yes, please. I'm looking for a sweatshirt.
Assistant: 2 ....
Emma: This dark blue one is nice. Can I try it on?
Assistant: 3 ....
Emma: Actually, I'm a medium. Have you got a bigger size?
Assistant: 4 ....
Emma: That's fine.
Assistant: 5 ....
Emma: It's great. How much is it?
Assistant: 6 ....
Emma: OK. I'll take it.

2 Jeremy wants some new walking boots. Complete the dialogue with the words in the box.

try cheaper are much size like
too better bigger ~~help~~

Assistant: Can I *help* you?
Jeremy: Yes. I'd 1 .... to see some walking boots, please.
Assistant: Of course. The sportswear is over there.
Jeremy: Excuse me. How 2 .... are these?
Assistant: They're £49.99.
Jeremy: Oh. They're a bit expensive.
Assistant: What about these? They're 3 ....
Jeremy: They're nice. Actually, I think they're a 4 .... colour than the first pair. Can I 5 .... them on?
Assistant: Yes, of course. What 6 .... are you?
Jeremy: I'm about a five.
Assistant: OK. Here you 7 .... How are they?
Jeremy: I'm afraid they're 8 .... small. Have you got a 9 .... size?
Assistant: Not at the moment – come back next week.

Listening

3 5.2 Listen to two dialogues and match them to the pictures (a, b or c). There is one extra picture.

Dialogue 1: ....
Dialogue 2: ....

4 Listen again and choose suitable expressions to continue the dialogues.

Thank you. Goodbye.
The ticket office closes at half past seven tonight.
Here you are.
Thanks. And here are your fish.
~~What time do you close?~~
OK. See you later.
~~That's £16, please.~~

Dialogue 1
A: *That's £16, please.*
B: ....
A: ....
B: ....

Dialogue 2
B: *What time do you close?*
A: ....
B: ....

Pronunciation: intonation in questions

5 5.3 Listen and repeat these questions.

1 Who's that girl?
2 What time is it?
3 Where is my geography book?
4 When does the concert start?
5 Why are you wearing walking boots?
6 How much is that sweatshirt?

Writing: a quiz

6 **Read the information from a website about the United Kingdom. Write the names of the countries and their capitals on the map.**

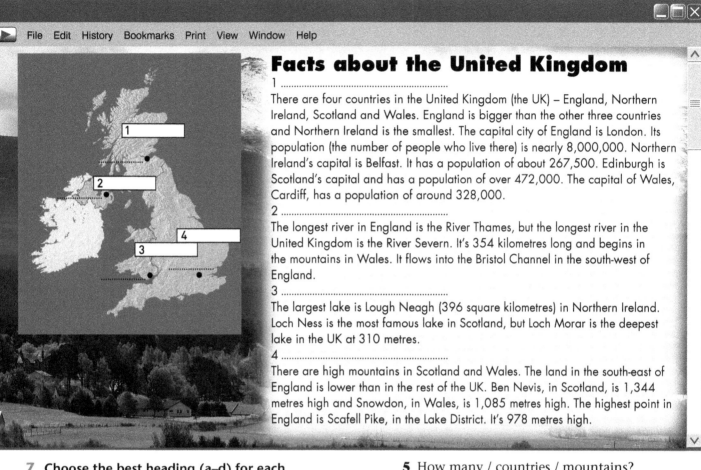

File Edit History Bookmarks Print View Window Help

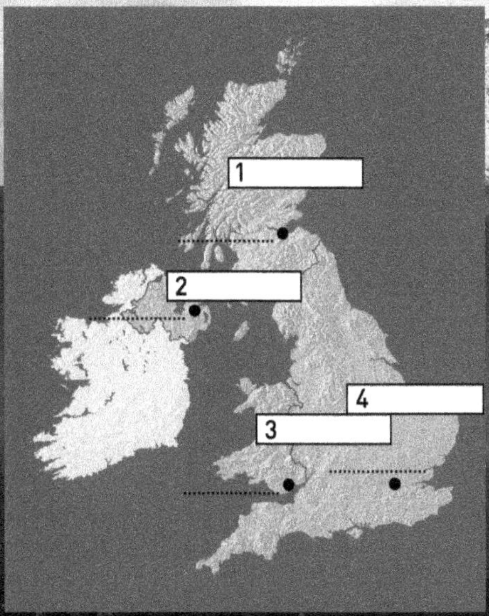

1 ....
2 ....
3 ....
4 ....

Facts about the United Kingdom

1 ....

There are four countries in the United Kingdom (the UK) – England, Northern Ireland, Scotland and Wales. England is bigger than the other three countries and Northern Ireland is the smallest. The capital city of England is London. Its population (the number of people who live there) is nearly 8,000,000. Northern Ireland's capital is Belfast. It has a population of about 267,500. Edinburgh is Scotland's capital and has a population of over 472,000. The capital of Wales, Cardiff, has a population of around 328,000.

2 ....

The longest river in England is the River Thames, but the longest river in the United Kingdom is the River Severn. It's 354 kilometres long and begins in the mountains in Wales. It flows into the Bristol Channel in the south-west of England.

3 ....

The largest lake is Lough Neagh (396 square kilometres) in Northern Ireland. Loch Ness is the most famous lake in Scotland, but Loch Morar is the deepest lake in the UK at 310 metres.

4 ....

There are high mountains in Scotland and Wales. The land in the south-east of England is lower than in the rest of the UK. Ben Nevis, in Scotland, is 1,344 metres high and Snowdon, in Wales, is 1,085 metres high. The highest point in England is Scafell Pike, in the Lake District. It's 978 metres high.

7 **Choose the best heading (a–d) for each paragraph (1–4). Write the headings in the text.**

a mountains **b** lakes **c** countries **d** rivers

8 **Write questions about the United Kingdom. Then choose the correct answer (a, b or c).**

How many / countries / the UK?

How many countries are there in the UK?

a three (**b** four) **c** five

1 Which / smallest / country / in the UK?

....

a Scotland **b** Northern Ireland **c** Wales

2 Which / longest river / in the UK?

....

a the River Thames **b** the River Trent **c** the River Severn

3 Where / longest river / begin?

....

a in Scotland **b** in Wales **c** in England

4 Which / deepest lake / in the UK?

....

a Lough Neagh **b** Loch Ness **c** Loch Morar

5 How many / countries / mountains?

....

a four **b** two **c** three

6 Which / highest mountain / in the UK?

....

a Ben Nevis **b** Snowdon **c** Scafell Pike

7 Where / lowest land / in the UK?

....

a in England **b** in Northern Ireland **c** in Scotland

9 **Write a quiz about your country. Make questions for the topics below. Give three possible answers for each question.**

the highest mountain	the most popular food
the longest river	the oldest building
the most famous person	the largest city

Try to think of questions with all the different question words: *what, which, where, when, how, how many, how much.*

5D Explore more

1 Read the website about South Africa. Match the answers (a–d) with the questions (1–3). There is one extra answer.

File Edit History Bookmarks Print View Window Help

South Africa: Facts and Figures

The highest point in the country is Champagne Castle. This is a mountain peak in the Drakensberg mountains. It is 3,375 m high.

The longest river in South Africa is the Orange River. It's about 2,100 km long. It begins in Lesotho (a country in the south of South Africa) and flows into the Atlantic Ocean in the northwest.

There is only one natural lake, called the Fundudzi Lake. The other lakes in South Africa are artificial. South Africa has 2,800 km of coastline.

The oldest national park is Kruger National Park. It covers an area of 19,485 square km and is also a reserve for wild animals.

1 How high is Champagne Castle?
2 How long is the Orange River?
3 How long is the coastline?

a 2,800 kilometres
b 2,100 kilometres
c 19,485 square kilometres
d 3,375 metres

2 Now do these exercises.

1 Match the answers (a–d) with the questions (1–3). There is one extra answer.

1 How tall are you?
2 How heavy are you?
3 What is your shoe size?

a I'm a size six.
b I'm fifty-eight kilogrammes.
c I'm 1 metre 54 centimetres.
d I'm thirty-six.

2 Match the answers (a–d) with the questions (1–3). There is one extra answer.

1 How much is this sweatshirt?
2 What size is this sweatshirt?
3 How much are these boots?

a They're a size five.
b It's £19.99.
c They're £39.99.
d It's a medium.

3 Match the answers (a–d) with the questions (1–3). There is one extra answer.

1 How is it?
2 What size are these trainers?
3 What size is this hat?

a It's a small.
b I'm afraid it's too small.
c It's £12.50.
d They're a size five.

Listening

3 5.4 **Listen to one of the dialogues on page 56 again. Choose the correct answer. You can listen to the dialogue twice.**

What does the boy want to do?

a buy fish for his dinner
b buy fish as pets
c buy a bigger fish tank

4 5.5 **Listen. What is the girl talking about? Choose the correct answer. You can listen twice.**

a her birthday
b a party
c her exams

5 5.6 **Listen to part of a radio programme. What is the man talking about? Choose the correct answer. You can listen twice.**

a the geography of Britain
b buildings and monuments in Britain
c the most famous castles in England

6 5.7 **Listen. What is the girl talking about? Choose the correct answer. You can listen twice.**

a her family
b a school trip to Wales
c a visit to Snowdon

Word list Unit 5

adult (n) ....
advantage (n) ....
ant (n) ....
antelope (n) ....
appetite (n) ....
attract (v) ....
average (n) ....
boat (n) ....
born (v) ....
brave (adj) ....
break off (phr v) ....
break up (phr v) ....
caver (n) ....
cheetah (n) ....
climber (n) ....
close (adj) ....
condition (n) ....
crab (n) ....
crew (n pl) ....
depend (v) ....
dig (v) ....
diabetes (n) ....
dive (v) ....
dry (adj) ....
elephant (n) ....
enough (adv) ....
equator (n) ....
expensive (adj) ....
experience (n) ....
extreme (adj) ....
fangs (n pl) ....
follow (v) ....
feet (n pl) ....
giant (n) ....
grow (v) ....
gun (n) ....
habitat (n) ....
hamster (n) ....
heavy (adj) ....
height (n) ....
helmet (n) ....
hostile (adj) ....
human (n) ....
incredible (adj) ....
inland (adj) ....
killer whale (n) ....
landscape (n) ....
large (adj) ....
leaf (n) ....
lion (n) ....
luckily (adv) ....
mad (adj) ....
other (adj) ....
painkiller (v) ....
pine tree (n) ....
plant (n) ....
prey (n) ....
quick (adj) ....
rabbit (n) ....
rainforest (n) ....
rattlesnake (n) ....
reef (n) ....
safe (adj) ....
savannah (n) ....
scared (adj) ....
slow (adj) ....
spine (n) ....
spit (v) ....
square (adj) ....
survive (v) ....
tentacles (n pl) ....
threaten (v) ....
through (adv) ....
tongue (n) ....
tortoise (n) ....
tough (adj) ....
trainers (n pl) ....
trekking (n) ....
try (*sth*) on (phr v) ....
underground (n) ....
violence (n) ....
warn (v) ....
web (n) ....
weigh (v) ....
wide (adj) ....

U5 Reading Explorer

crab (n) ....
diabetes (n) ....
fangs (n pl) ....
painkiller (v) ....
prey (n) ....
rattlesnake (n) ....
spine (n) ....
spit (v) ....
tentacles (n pl) ....
threaten (v) ....
warn (v) ....
web (n) ....

Grammar Practice Unit 5

Comparative adjectives

We use **comparative adjectives** to compare two people, animals or things. We form the comparative with **adjective** + ***-er*** + ***than*** or ***more/ less*** + **adjective** + ***than.***

*A hippopotamus is **bigger** than a horse.*

*A shark is **more dangerous** than an antelope.*

*English is **less difficult** than Chinese.*

- **adjectives with one syllable**

  With one-syllable adjectives, we form the comparative by adding *-er*.

  tall – **taller**

  If the adjective ends in *-e*, we just add *-r*.

  nice – **nicer**

  If the adjective ends in a **single vowel + consonant**, we double the consonant and add *-er*.

  big – **bigger**

- **adjectives with** ***-y***

  With adjectives ending in *-y*, we change the *-y* to *-ier*.

  dry – **drier** heavy – **heavier**

- **adjectives with two or more syllables**

  With other adjectives of two or more syllables, we form the comparative by adding ***more*** or ***less*** before the adjective.

  boring – **more/less** boring

  exciting – **more/less** exciting

  interesting – **more/less** interesting

- **irregular adjectives**

  good – **better**

  bad – **worse**

  many, much – **more**

  a lot of, lots of – **more**

  little – **less**

1 Write sentences with the comparative form + *than*.

Elephants are *bigger than* dogs. (**big**)

1 Dogs are .... cats. (**friendly**)

2 Snakes are .... tortoises. (**fast**)

3 A hamster is .... a mouse. (**fat**)

4 Crocodiles are .... cows. (**dangerous**)

5 An elephant is .... a shark. (**heavy**)

6 Gorillas are .... zebras. (**intelligent**)

2 Write the adjectives from the box, with their comparative forms, in the correct part of the table.

bad	brave	fantastic	funny
good	~~hot~~	many	playful
poisonous	scary	small	ugly

1 syllable	ending in 'y'	2+ syllables	irregular
....	....	....	....
hot - hotter	....	....	....
....	....	....	....

3 Write sentences with the comparative form with these words.

sharks / small / elephants.

Sharks are smaller than elephants.

1 Spain / hot / the UK.

....

2 gorillas / interesting / rabbits.

....

3 deserts / dry / river deltas.

....

4 crocodiles / ugly / sharks.

....

5 bears / dangerous / mice.

....

4 Write questions with the comparative form with these words.

a mouse / dangerous / a lion?

Is a mouse more dangerous than a lion?

1 the Pacific Ocean / big / the Atlantic Ocean?

....

2 mountains / high / valleys?

....

3 rabbits / friendly / tortoises?

....

4 having money / good / being happy?

....

5 your friends / important / your family?

....

too and *not enough*

We use ***too*** + **adjective** or ***not*** + **adjective** + ***enough*** to explain why something is/was not possible.

Why can't Adam drive a car?

He's **too young**. [young = not old]
He **isn't old enough.**

5 Write two sentences for each statement. Use *too* and *enough*.

Why didn't you answer Question 6? (difficult / easy)

It was *too difficult.*

It *wasn't easy enough.*

1 Why didn't they buy that car? (expensive / cheap)

It was ....

It ....

2 Can your little sister open the top window? (short / tall)

No, she can't. She's ....

No, she can't. She ....

3 Why can't I watch that movie? (young / old)

You're ....

You ....

4 Why didn't you swim in the sea? (cold / warm)

It was ....

It ....

Superlative adjectives

We use **superlative adjectives** to compare one person, animal or thing with two or more others. We form the superlative with ***the*** + **adjective** + ***-est*** or ***the most/least*** + **adjective**.

- **adjectives with one syllable**

  With one-syllable adjectives, we form the superlative by adding ***the ...-est***.

  cold – **the** cold**est**

  With adjectives ending in a **single vowel** + **consonant**, we double the consonant and add ***the ...-est***.

  hot – **the** hott**est**

- **adjectives with** *-y*

  With adjectives ending in *-y*, we change the *-y* to ***the ...-iest***.

  dry – **the** dr**iest** ugly – **the** ugl**iest**

- **adjectives with two or more syllables**

  With other adjectives of two or more syllables, we form the superlative by adding ***the most*** or ***the least*** before the adjective.

  famous – **the most/least** famous

  important – **the most/least** important

- **irregular adjectives**

  There are some irregular adjectives that don't follow the rules above.

  good – **the best**

  bad – **the worst**

  many, much – **the most**

  a lot of, lots of – **the most**

  a little – **the least**

6 Write sentences with the superlative form of the words in brackets.

Giraffes are *the tallest* animals of all. (**tall**)

1 Lake Titicaca is .... lake in the world. (**high**)

2 Shakespeare is .... writer of all time. (**famous**)

3 This is one of .... places on Earth. (**dry**)

4 It was .... hurricane in the last fifty years. (**bad**)

5 *Jaws* was .... film of its time. (**successful**)

have to

We use ***have to*** to talk about what is/isn't necessary.

*Musicians **have to** practise a lot.*

We form the affirmative with ***have/has to*** + the bare infinitive of the main verb.

*Vets **have to** love animals.*

*A doctor **has to** do years of special training.*

We form the **negative** with ***don't/doesn't*** + ***have to*** + the bare infinitive of the main verb.

*We **don't have to** wear school uniform on school trips.*

*Adam **doesn't have to** go to bed early on Friday.*

7 Complete the sentences with *have to/has to* (✔) or *don't have to/doesn't have to* (✘).

I *don't have to* get up early today – it's Sunday! (✘)

1 Fire fighters .... do special training. (✔)

2 Our teacher said we .... study today. (✘)

3 Judy .... finish her homework before she goes out. (✔)

4 Mum .... make me lunch – I always eat at school. (✘)

5 We .... be at the cinema by eight o'clock. (✔)

We make questions by putting ***Do/Does*** before the subject, and then ***have to*** + the bare infinitive of the main verb.

***Do** I/you/we/they **have to** buy my brother a present?*

***Does** a bus driver **have to** pass a test?*

In short answers we use ***do/don't*** or ***does/doesn't***. We DON'T use the main verb.

8 Write questions with these words and the correct form of *have to*, then write affirmative (✔) and negative (✘) short answers.

we / learn English? (✔)

Do we have to learn English? Yes, you do.

1 Kate / study for a Spanish test? (✔)

....

2 farmers / wear a uniform? (✘)

....

3 you / tidy your room? (✔)

....

4 a basketball player / wear a helmet? (✘)

....

5 you and your sister / visit your grandparents? (✔)

....

6A Desert racing

Vocabulary: sports and games

1 Read the clues and complete the sports crossword.

Across

1 This game is very popular in England and Australia. The players wear white clothes.

4 To win you must hit the ball into a hole in the ground. You mustn't hit it too many times.

6 Two or four players hit a small ball against a wall in this very fast-moving game.

9 You play indoors. There's a high net and you need rackets, but you don't use a ball.

11 You can play this team game inside or outside. You use your hands to hit the ball.

12 This is a popular game in Europe and America. The players are usually very tall.

Down

2 This sport is one of the most dangerous team games. The ball is oval-shaped.

3 You play this with small bats and a large table with a net across the middle.

5 This is a popular sport in America. The players hit the ball and run round the field.

7 This is the most popular sport in the world. You need eleven players to make a team.

8 This is a ball game you play inside. You play in a team and you can use your hands to score a goal.

10 You play this team game on a field. The ball is very hard and the players hit the ball across the ground with hard sticks.

Grammar: *must* and *must not* (*mustn't*)

2 Write the rules with *must* or *mustn't*.

You / feed the animals / at the zoo

You mustn't feed the animals at the zoo.

1 You / go near the animals / at the zoo

....

2 You / wear / sun cream / on the beach

....

3 You / talk / during an exam

....

4 You / use your mobile phone / in the library

....

5 Cyclists and skaters / use the bikeway

....

6 Walkers and runners / use the walkway

....

7 You / take photos / in the museum

....

Grammar: *can/can't* and *must/mustn't*

3 Complete the rules for the sports and games. Circle the correct option.

Football

1 Players *mustn't / can* touch the ball with their hands.

2 The goalkeeper *must / can* use his hands to stop the ball.

3 Players *can / must* wear football boots.

Chess

4 At the beginning of the game, you *can / must* try to take control of the centre of the board.

5 During the game, you *can / mustn't* take the other player's pieces.

6 After you move a piece, you *can't / must* put it back.

Working with words: verbs – nouns

4 Complete the table.

Verb	Nouns	
compete	*competition*	competitor
....	exploration	....
....	....	inventor
investigate	....	....
....	....	celebrator
imagine	....	
prepare	....	

5 Complete the sentences with words from the table in Exercise 4. Make the words plural where necessary.

Before you *compete* in a race, you must do warm-up exercises.

1. Russian players often win international chess ....
2. The police finished their .... yesterday.
3. I think Picasso had more .... than Van Gogh.
4. Did you have a party to .... New Year?
5. John Logie Baird was a famous .... He built the first television.
6. Marco Polo was a famous Italian .... who travelled to China and Mongolia.
7. Teachers have to do a lot of .... before their classes.

Vocabulary: food

6 Match the pictures (1–13) with the words (a–m).

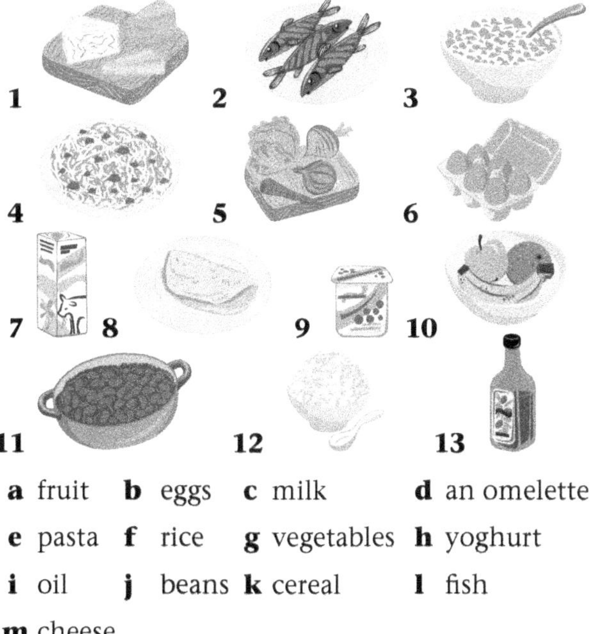

a fruit **b** eggs **c** milk **d** an omelette
e pasta **f** rice **g** vegetables **h** yoghurt
i oil **j** beans **k** cereal **l** fish
m cheese

7 Complete the sentences with words from Exercise 6.

1. Most English people eat a bowl of .... for breakfast.
2. Cows produce ....
3. .... and .... also come from cows.
4. The French are famous for their ...., such as Roquefort and Camembert.
5. Olive .... is great on salad. Spanish people put it on bread, too.
6. Chinese people eat .... every day.
7. You need .... to make a(n) ....

8 Complete the puzzle to find the hidden phrase.

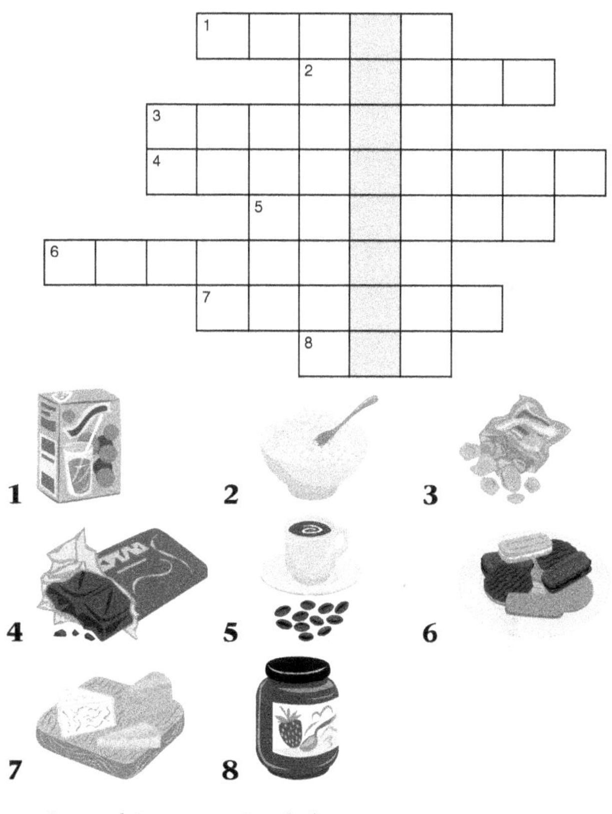

Something very English: ....

9 Match the food items with their containers in the box. You can match some items with more than one container.

jar bottle can / tin box carton packet cup

1. milk *bottle, carton, cup*
2. sardines ....
3. rice ....
4. yoghurt ....
5. juice ....
6. coffee ....
7. chocolate ....
8. cereal ....
9. eggs ....
10. crisps ....
11. beans ....
12. water ....
13. biscuits ....
14. tea ....

6B Expedition food

Listening

1 **6.1 Listen to the interview with an expert on hiking and trekking and match the activities (1–3) with the photos (a–c).**

1 walking ....
2 hiking ....
3 trekking ....

a

b

c

2 **Listen again. Are the sentences true or false?**

	T	F
You can go walking in a town.	✓	☐
1 You can go hiking on your own.	☐	☐
2 You can't take children hiking.	☐	☐
3 Trekkers usually walk on roads and paths.	☐	☐
4 Hikers sometimes carry a tent.	☐	☐
5 Trekkers often climb mountains.	☐	☐
6 Trekking takes longer than hiking.	☐	☐
7 Trekkers and hikers have different equipment.	☐	☐

Grammar: countable and uncountable nouns

3 **Look at the underlined words. Write *C* for countable nouns and *U* for uncountable nouns.**

Trekkers need to take <u>a backpack</u> with them. ..C..

1 They also need to take some <u>food</u>. ....
2 Have we got any <u>biscuits</u>? ....
3 There's no <u>rice</u> in the cupboard. ....
4 Did you buy any <u>fish</u>? ....
5 I'd love <u>a cup of coffee</u>! ....
6 I've got some <u>eggs</u> in the fridge. .... Would you like <u>an omelette</u>? ....
7 Can I have some <u>sugar</u> in my .... <u>tea</u>, please? ....

4 **Complete the sentences with *a*, *an* or – (no article).**

1 Can I have .... bottle of water, please?
2 Do you like .... sardines?
3 Can you pass me .... orange, please?
4 There was .... carton of juice on the table.
5 In Asia, people eat .... rice every day.
6 They don't eat .... cheese.

5 **Complete the text with *some*, *any* or *no*.**

Last winter I went hiking with some friends in the Welsh mountains. There wasn't [1] .... snow on the ground, but it was very cold! On the first day, we walked for three hours then we stopped and had [2] .... hot tea and cake. The cold and the exercise made me very hungry and I wished I had [3] .... chocolate with me! I didn't have [4] .... gloves with me on the first day, so my hands got really cold. We walked through a village in the afternoon and I wanted to buy [5] .... gloves, but I realised I had [6] .... money with me. On the second day, I wore gloves and three pairs of socks and it was much better. The mountains were very beautiful. We walked all day and we didn't see [7] .... people and there were almost [8] .... cars on the roads. I've got [9] .... photos of the trip in my room. Do you want to see them?

6 **Complete the sentences with *a lot of*, *much* or *many*.**

1 How .... did your new walking boots cost?
2 I don't know how .... pairs of socks to take.
3 He always has .... money. I think he's quite rich.
4 How .... people went on the trip with you?
5 Tell me how .... pasta you want.
6 I usually drink .... water.

Reading

7 Read the text and choose the best heading (a–d) for each paragraph (1–4).

a A strange meal
b The end of a long journey
c From west to east
d Alone on the wall

Walking the wall

1 ....

The Great Wall of China is about 4,000 kilometres long and was built by the Chinese to protect their northern villages from attackers. Today, many parts of the wall are in ruins but some parts of the wall are solid and you can walk along the top. In the year 2000, a Maori lawyer, Nathan Hoturoa Gray, and four other hikers from different countries decided to walk from the western end of the wall to the eastern end. This is where the wall meets the sea at Laolong Kou, which means 'Head of the Dragon'.

2 ....

After about a month of walking and trekking across mountains, deserts and icy rivers, Nathan found himself alone. The other members of the group couldn't continue because they were ill or injured. Nathan wanted to continue but he didn't have any food or water. He needed to find a village, but the tiny villages weren't on any of his maps. Luckily, he saw a small village down in a valley. When he reached the village, he pulled out his water bottle and a young boy ran inside his hut and came back with some water.

3 ....

The people in the village were very poor, but the boy's parents invited Nathan to stay and eat some food with them. First, the family gave him a jar of tea leaves, some apples, biscuits and bread. Then they offered him some hot noodles, some fried crickets, and some pigs' ears! He was so hungry that he ate the food very fast. It tasted great.

4 ....

Nathan was ready to continue his journey, so he thanked the villagers and left. He met many other helpful Chinese people along the way. After many months of walking with blisters on his feet, and many nights with no sleep, he finally arrived at the Head of the Dragon.

8 Read the text again and choose the correct option (a, b or c).

The Great Wall of China:
a is 4,000 years old.
b is completely ruined.
c was built to stop attackers.

1 The group of hikers:
a started their walk at Laolong Kou.
b trekked across wild habitats.
c were all Maoris.

2 The other four hikers left Nathan to continue alone because:
a they became ill or had accidents.
b they didn't like him.
c he didn't walk fast enough.

3 When Nathan arrived in the village, the young boy:
a ran away because he was frightened.
b went inside his hut.
c stole Nathan's water bottle.

4 What did Nathan eat?
a He ate everything including pigs' ears.
b He ate some noodles, but he didn't eat any pigs' ears.
c He didn't eat the crickets, but he ate everything else.

5 After Nathan left the village:
a he didn't meet any more people.
b he met lots of other people who helped him.
c he saw a Chinese dragon festival.

9 Complete the sentences about Nathan's journey. Check your answers in the text.

1 Nathan didn't have any .... in his bottle.
2 Nathan needed to find a village because he had no ....
3 The villages weren't on any of his ....
4 The boy's family gave him a jar of ....
5 Then, they gave him some ...., ... and ....
6 Sometimes Nathan had no .... at night.

6C Permission

Asking for permission

1 Match the questions (1–4) with the responses (a–d).

1 Can I ask you a question?
2 Can I stay at Jake's house tonight?
3 Can't I go later?
4 Do I have to have tea with you?

a Yes, you do.
b OK, but you must spend some time with her first.
c No, I'm afraid you can't. Your grandmother is coming tonight.
d Yes, of course.

2 Now complete the dialogue with the words in the box.

do	can't (x2)	ask	can (x4)	must	course	have

Ruby: Mum, can I [1] .... you a question?
Mum: Yes, of course you can, Ruby. What is it?
Ruby: Well, you know when Holly comes tomorrow …
Mum: Yes …
Ruby: Well, [2] .... we go into town?
Mum: Yes, of [3] ....
Ruby: [4] .... we go on the bus?
Mum: OK, but you [5] .... be back by 4.00.
Ruby: But, we can't go to the cinema if we come back so early! Do we [6] .... to?
Mum: Yes, you [7] .... It's not safe to be out in the city late at night.
Ruby: But we wanted to see the new James Bond film.
Mum: You [8] .... go to the cinema in the afternoon.
Ruby: But we wanted to go shopping in the afternoon. [9] .... we go to the cinema in the evening?
Mum: No, I'm afraid you [10] .... Why don't you go on Sunday? Dad [11] .... take you.
Ruby: OK. Thanks, Mum.

3 Complete the dialogue with questions and responses in the box.

- Oh no! I haven't got a printer at home!
- Do we have to do all the exercises on page 34 – they're really difficult!
- Yes, of course. Good idea! Thanks.
- OK. Thanks. Can I ask a question about the history project?
- Do we have to type it and print it out, or can we hand in a written copy?
- Hi Tom. Can you help me? I don't understand the homework.

Emily: [1] ....
Tom: Yes, of course. What's the problem?
Emily: [2] ....
Tom: No, we don't. We only have to read the text and answer the first two questions.
Emily: [3] ....
Tom: Yeah. Sure.
Emily: [4] ....
Tom: I'm afraid we have to hand in a printed copy.
Emily: [5] ....
Tom: No, we can't. Can't you go to the library in town and use their printer?
Emily: [6] ....
Tom: You're welcome.

4 Look at the library rules and complete the dialogue with suitable expressions from Exercises 1, 2 and 3.

Emily: Hello. [1] .... use a computer, please?
Librarian: Yes, [2] .... Here's your access code.
Emily: Thanks. [3] .... use my own paper?
Librarian: [4] .... afraid. You must use library paper.
Emily: [5] Do I .... pay for it?
Librarian: Yes, [6] .... It's 5p a sheet.
Emily: OK. Thanks.

COMPUTER ROOM

open
Monday - Saturday
from
9.00 a.m. - 5.30 p.m.

Ask the librarian for access codes and printer paper

5 Make requests for the situations below. Use the correct expressions in the box.

go home early	open the window
have some more lemonade	~~have a party~~
copy yours	borrow your scarf
give him some fish	borrow some money

It's my birthday next week. *Can I have a party?*

1 I need to buy a sandwich.
2 I'm thirsty!
3 I didn't understand the maths homework.
4 It's really cold outside.
5 The cat's hungry.
6 It's very hot in here.
7 I'm not feeling very well.

Pronunciation: /s/ and /z/

6 6.2 **Say the pairs of words and write /s/ or /z/ next to each word. Listen and check.**

1 ice	....	eyes	....
2 rays	....	race	....
3 rice	....	rise	....
4 prize	....	price	....
5 chess	....	cheese	....
6 apples	....	biscuits	....

Writing: a report

7 Jay wrote about his favourite restaurant for the school magazine. Read the text and answer the questions.

1 What kind of restaurant is it?
2 Why does he like it so much?
3 When does he go to Manolo's?
4 When and why did he last go there?
5 Did his grandparents like the food at Manolo's?

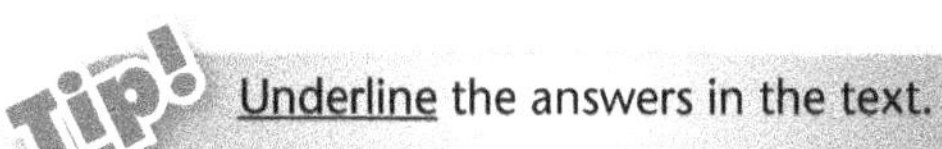

8 Read the poster and choose one of the topics.

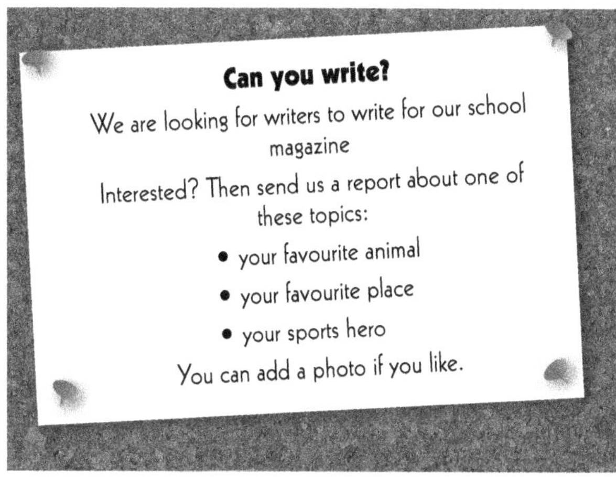

Can you write?
We are looking for writers to write for our school magazine
Interested? Then send us a report about one of these topics:
• your favourite animal
• your favourite place
• your sports hero
You can add a photo if you like.

9 Plan your paragraph. Write notes in answer to the questions. Use the linking words in the box.

and	because	but	so	when

1 What is your favourite animal, place or sports hero?
2 Why? What things do you like the most about him / her / it?
3 When was the last time you went there or saw him / her?
4 What happened?

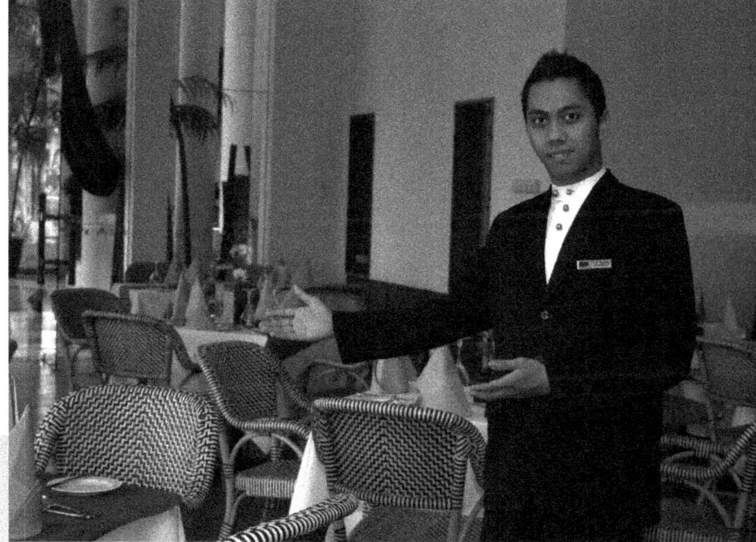

My favourite restaurant

I love Spanish food, so I always go to Manolo's, the Spanish restaurant down the road, when it's my birthday. My family love the food at Manolo's, so we go there every time we have a celebration.

They make a special kind of paella from Valencia. It's made with rice, vegetables and fish, but they also put some potatoes in it. Two years ago I went to Spain on holiday and I think Manolo's paella is better than the ones I had in Spain. I also like the people who work there. They're all Spanish and they're very friendly. And it's not too expensive!

The last time I went there was in June. My older brother passed all his exams and got a place at university, so we went there to celebrate. Last summer my grandparents came to visit from India so we took them to Manolo's. They only eat Indian food, so they didn't want to be too adventurous. They just ordered beans and rice, but they loved it!

Jay Singh Rai

6D Explore more

Reading

1 Match the signs (a–c) with the places (1–4). There is one extra place.

1 school
2 museum
3 national park
4 safari park

2 Now do these exercises.

1 Match the signs (a–c) with the places (1–4). There is one extra place.

1 a restaurant
2 in a library
3 in a shoe shop
4 in a supermarket

2 Match the signs (a–c) with the places (1–4). There is one extra place.

1 in a shop
2 on a plane
3 in the street
4 in a sports centre

3 Match the signs (a–c) with the places (1–4). There is one extra place.

1 on a bus
2 in a park
3 in a theatre
4 in a sports shop

3 Complete the dialogue with the responses (a–c). There is one extra response.

A: Where's your project, Anna?
B: 1 ....
A: Well, you know the deadline is today.
B: 2 ....
A: No, sorry. You must hand it in before 3 o'clock today.

a No, I didn't finish it.
b Can't I hand it in tomorrow?
c Sorry. I haven't got it.

4 Complete the dialogues (1–3) with the responses (a–c). There is one extra response.

1

A: I'm bored! What can I do?
B: 1 ....
A: Really? That's great, Mum. Thanks!
B: 2 ....

a Why don't you invite your friends here?
b I'm not sure.
c You're welcome!

2

A: Can I use the printer?
B: 1 ....
A: Thanks. Have you got any printer paper?
B: 2 ....
A: OK. I'll come back later.

a No, you can't.
b Yes, of course.
c No, students have to bring their own paper.

3

A: Can I have some juice, please?
B: 1 ....
A: OK. Can I have a bottle of water then, please?
B: 2 ....
A: Here you are.

a Yes. That's £1.20, please.
b Why don't you go to the shop?
c I'm afraid I haven't got any juice.

Word list Unit 6

(be) afraid of (phr) ....
access (n) ....
accident (n) ....
altitude (n) ....
attach (v) ....
bean (n) ....
beat (n) ....
biscuit (n) ....
bitter (adj) ....
blood (n) ....
bottom (n) ....
breathe (n) ....
bridge (n) ....
camp (v) ....
carbon dioxide (n) ....
celebrate (v) ....
cereal (n) ....
climb (v) ....
compare (v) ....
competitor (n) ....
conversation (n) ....
cord (n) ....
cough sweets (n pl) ....
crack open (phr) ....
cricket (n) ....
crisps (n pl) ....
crush (v) ....
darts (n pl) ....
deadline (n) ....
descent (n) ....
distant (adj) ....
diabetes (n) ....
dragon (n) ....
draughts (pl) ....
drop (v) ....
equipment (n) ....
excellent (adj) ....
extremely (adv) ....
feed (v) ....
formation (n) ....
grains (n pl) ....
glacier (n) ....
grind (v) ....
hand in (phr v) ....
harvest (n) ....
harbour (n) ....
harness (n) ....
heartbeat (n) ....
heritage (n) ....
hiker (n) ....
hiking (n) ....
imagine (v) ....
include (v) ....
injured (adj) ....
jar (n) ....
lend (v) ....
librarian (n) ....
litter (n) ....
lung (n) ....
muscle (n) ....
noodles (n) ....
official (n) ....
onion (n) ....
order (v) ....
oxygen (n) ....
packet (n) ....
pasta (n) ....
permission (n) ....
piece (n) ....
powdered (adj) ....
powder (n) ....
prepare (v) ....
printing press (n) ....
processed food (n) ....
pull out (phr v) ....
pump (v) ....
race (n) ....
rice (n) ....
rock (n) ....
roast (v) ....
rope (n) ....
sandwich (n) ....
shades (n pl) ....
sheet (n) ....
skater (n) ....
skydiving (n) ....
slow down (phr v) ....
soil (n) ....
squeeze (v) ....
stalks (n pl) ....
sticky mass (phr) ....
sugarcane (n) ....
sunburnt (adj) ....
surface (n) ....
syrup (n) ....
terrifying (adj) ....
thirsty (adj) ....
top (n) ....
touch (v) ....
trekker (n) ....
twice (adv) ....
valley (n) ....
villager (n) ....
walkway (n) ....
waterfall (n) ....
wish (v) ....
wrist (n) ....

U6 Reading Explorer

bitter (adj) ....
crack open (phr) ....
crush (v) ....
diabetes (n) ....
grains (n pl) ....
grind (v) ....
harvest (n) ....
powder (n) ....
processed food (n) ....
roast (v) ....
shades (n pl) ....
soil (n) ....
squeeze (v) ....
stalks (n pl) ....
sticky mass (phr) ....
sugarcane (n) ....
syrup (n) ....

Grammar Practice Unit 6

must/mustn't

We use ***must*** to talk about what the rules/laws/ etc tell us to do.

*You **must** wear a helmet on a motorbike.*

Must has the same form for all subjects (*I, you, he,* etc). The main verb after ***must*** is in the **bare infinitive.**

*I/We/She/etc **must** go to school.*

The negative of ***must*** is ***mustn't*** *(must not)* and it is the same for all subjects.

> ***Mustn't*** does NOT mean something is not necessary; it means something is against the rules/law (i.e. not permitted).
> *You **don't have to** cycle to school – you can walk.* (It's not necessary.)
> *You **mustn't** cycle on the walkway.* (It is not permitted.)

1 Complete the school rules with *must* or *mustn't*.

You *mustn't* write on the walls.

1 You .... do your homework.
2 You .... make a noise in class.
3 You .... walk on the grass. Use the footpaths.
4 You .... wear the correct school uniform.
5 You .... do what the teachers say.
6 You .... be late for a lesson.
7 You .... always be polite.
8 You .... use your mobile phone in class.

2 Write sentences about these signs and notices using *must* or *mustn't*.

No photography (in a museum)
You mustn't take photos in the museum.

1 No swimming (at a dangerous beach)

....

2 Please do not feed the animals (at a zoo)

....

3 Please switch off mobile phones (in a theatre)

....

4 No ball games (in a park)

....

5 Keep car windows closed (in a safari park)

....

6 No talking (in a library)

....

7 Please do not speak to the driver (on a bus)

....

8 No parking (on a street)

....

3 Choose the correct words.

You *mustn't* / ~~*don't have to*~~ go near the animals. They are dangerous.

1 The train leaves at 6:00. You *mustn't / don't have to* get to the station at 5:30.
2 You *mustn't / don't have to* forget to bring your history projects tomorrow.
3 The coach *mustn't / doesn't have to* choose the team now. He can decide on Friday.
4 This homework is for next week. I *mustn't / don't have to* finish it today.
5 Put your bikes behind the school. You *mustn't / don't have to* leave them here.
6 You *mustn't / don't have to* lock your bikes at school – but it's a good idea to do it.

4 Complete the sentences with *must, mustn't, doesn't have to* or *don't have to*.

You *must* be at the airport at least an hour before your plane leaves.

1 You .... be quiet – the baby's sleeping.
2 We .... cook tonight – we can order a pizza.
3 You .... skateboard here. Look – that sign says so.
4 Kenny .... sing in the school concert, but he wants to.
5 You .... wear a helmet on a motorbike. It's the law.

can/can't and *must/mustn't*

We use ***can*** to ask what is/isn't permitted; in short answers we use ***can*** or ***can't***.

***Can** I use my mobile phone in the aeroplane?*
*- No, you **can't**. You **mustn't** use it here. You **must** switch it off.*
***Can** I eat my sandwiches here?*
*- No, you **can't**. You **mustn't** eat in the library.*

5 Choose the correct words.

You ~~*can*~~ / *mustn't* be careless with library books.

1 You *can't / must* follow the library rules.
2 To borrow a library book, you *can't / must* first be a member of the library.
3 You *can / mustn't* become a member quickly and easily.
4 Members *can / must* borrow a library book for up to one week.
5 You *can / mustn't* eat, drink or talk in the library.
6 You *can / must* find books here about anything you're interested in.

Countable and uncountable nouns

Countable nouns are nouns we can count – e.g. *one **camera*** (singular), *two **cameras*** (plural). When the subject is plural, the verb is also plural.

*This **tent** is too small.* *These **boots** are too big.*

Uncountable nouns are nouns we can't count (***food**, **milk***, etc). They haven't got a plural form. When the subject is an uncountable noun, the verb is singular.

*The **water** was very cold.*

We DON'T use ***a*** or ***an*** with uncountable nouns or plural nouns.

We can use countable words like a ***piece***, a **bottle**, a ***cup***, a ***glass***, a ***carton***, etc to show how much there is of something uncountable.

*We need a **carton** of orange juice.*

*Two **cups** of coffee, please!*

6 Write the words in the correct part of the table.

~~apple~~	biscuit	bottle	~~bread~~	burger
carton	cheese	chocolate	cup	egg
fruit	milk	oil	packet	pasta	rice
sandwich	sugar	tin	water	

Countable		Uncountable	
apple	....	*bread*	....
....	....	....	....
....	....	....	....
....	....	....	....
....	....	....	....

7 Complete the sentences with *a*, *an* or – (no article).

Are we having – pasta for dinner again?

1 Do you want .... biscuit with your tea?
2 'What do you want to drink?' 'Oh, just .... water, thanks.'
3 I had .... carton of yoghurt for breakfast.
4 Do you like .... oil on your salad?
5 I often have .... apple with my lunch.
6 I'd like .... omelette, please.

some, *any* and *no*

In **affirmative** sentences, we use ***some*** before countable nouns in the plural and before uncountable nouns.

*There were **some** eggs in the fridge.*

*There was **some** oil in the bottle.*

In **negative** sentences and **questions**, we use ***any*** before countable nouns in the plural and before uncountable nouns.

*We didn't see **any** animals in the desert.*

*We didn't take **any** food with us.*

*Did you see **any** lions at the zoo?*

*Were there **any** pictures on the walls?*

*Did you have **any** water in your water bottle?*

In negative sentences, we can use ***no*** in the same way as ***not any***.

*There were **no** TVs 100 years ago.*

*I had **no** money to buy food.*

8 Complete the sentences with *was, wasn't, were* or *weren't*.

There ...*were*... some apples in the fruit bowl.

1 Did you finish the cheese? There .... some on this plate five minutes ago.
2 There .... any nice oranges at the supermarket today.
3 It was very quiet in the park. There .... no other people there.
4 I wanted a sandwich but there .... any bread.
5 I wanted a milkshake but there .... no milk.
6 I wanted an omelette but there .... any eggs.

9 Complete the sentences with *some, any* or *no*.

We haven't got .*any*. rice.

1 We have to get ...... milk.
2 You can't drive across the desert because there are ...... roads there.
3 I didn't put ...... sugar in your tea.
4 I didn't make a cheese omelette because there was ...... cheese.
5 I ate ...... fruit and a sandwich for lunch.
6 Were there ...... phone calls for me today?
7 Let's get ...... fish and chips for dinner.
8 There aren't ...... tigers in Africa.

10 Complete the sentences in the affirmative or negative. Use the past simple form of the verbs.

We ...*took*... (take) some biscuits with us.

We ...*didn't carry*... (carry) any heavy equipment.

1 There .... (be) no signs, so we didn't know where to go.
2 We .... (have) any maps with us, either.
3 We .... (see) some cows in a field.
4 We .... (see) any other animals.
5 I was thirsty, but we .... (have) no water in our water bottles.
6 It was very hot too, but there .... (be) any trees to sit under.
7 I .... (take) some photos of us at the top of the hill.
8 We .... (find) any pirate treasure.

Review Units 5 and 6

1 Choose the correct option to complete the sentences.

1 I'm hungry. Have you got *a / any* bread?
2 There *is some / are some* eggs in the fridge.
3 I can't make a cake. I've got *no / any* sugar.
4 Excuse me? I'd like *some / any* information about English courses, please.
5 Did you eat *all the / every* biscuits?
6 How *many / much* people were there at the party?
7 I ate *a lot of / many* chocolate. Now I feel ill!
8 There isn't *any / a* furniture in the room.
9 How *much / many* money have you got?
10 Let's watch *a / one* DVD tonight.

1 mark per item: ... / 10 marks

2 Complete the sentences with *some, any* or *no*.

1 Did you buy .... cheese?
2 They didn't have .... biscuits.
3 We saw .... people in the park.
4 He didn't see the museum because he had .... time.
5 I had .... chocolate. It was delicious.
6 There wasn't .... bread in the kitchen.
7 Let's buy .... oranges.
8 The fruit bowl was empty. There was .... fruit in it.
9 They didn't have .... milk.
10 There was .... sugar in my tea. It was very sweet.

1 mark per item: ... / 10 marks

3 Complete the sentences with the comparative or superlative forms of the adjectives in brackets.

1 England is .... Wales. (large)
2 Gold earrings are .... silver earrings. (expensive)
3 Ben Nevis is .... mountain in Britain. (high)
4 John's exam result is .... Brad's. (bad)
5 I think physics is .... maths. (boring)
6 Sandra is .... singer in the class. (good)
7 Australia is .... New Zealand. (hot)
8 I think Paris is .... city in the world. (beautiful)
9 I think biology is .... chemistry. (interesting)
10 Riding a motorbike is .... driving a car. (dangerous)

2 marks per item: ... / 20 marks

4 Write the sentences using *too* or *enough*.

1 I / short / to play basketball.
....
2 Fiona / not strong / to carry that suitcase.
....
3 Be careful. The river / dangerous / to cross.
....
4 My friends / scared / to watch the horror film.
....
5 It / not hot / to swim in the sea.
....

1 mark per item: ... / 5 marks

5 Rewrite the sentences using *must, mustn't* or *can*.

1 Don't feed the animals at the zoo.
You ....
2 Turn your mobile phone off during the exam.
You ....
3 It's OK to take your dog to this park.
You ....
4 Don't wear shoes in the house.
You ....
5 This film is for children over 15.
Children over ....

1 mark per item: ... / 5 marks

6 Write the names of the animals.

1 This animal is sometimes poisonous.
s..............................

2 This animal is 'the king of the jungle'.
l..............................

3 This large fish can kill you.
s..............................

4 They have black and white stripes.
z..............................

5 They carry their house on their backs.
t..............................

6 It's the fastest animal on Earth.
c..............................

7 It has lots of teeth and is dangerous.
c..............................

8 It's big and heavy, and has short legs.
h..............................

1 mark per item: ... / 8 marks

7 Label the pictures of habitats.

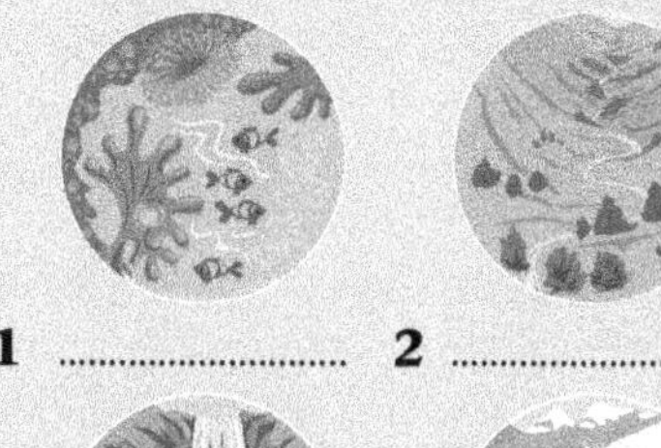

1 .... **2** .... **3** ....

4 .... **5** .... **6** ....

1 mark per item: ... / 6 marks

8 Write the sports and games.

1 .... **2** .... **3** ....

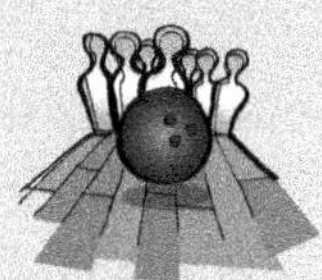

4 .... **5** ....

2 marks per item: ... / 10 marks

9 Complete the sentences with the words in the box.

cereal crisps cup eggs fish jam lemonade pasta rice vegetables

1 You need .... to make a cake.

2 Onions, potatoes and green beans are all ....

3 I usually have a bowl of .... for breakfast.

4 My favourite .... are cheese and onion.

5 It's traditional to eat .... on Fridays.

6 I sometimes have a(n) .... of tea in the afternoon.

7 The Chinese eat a lot of ....

8 My favourite food is ...., especially spaghetti.

9 My grandmother makes .... with lemons, water and sugar.

10 You make .... with fruit and sugar.

2 marks per item: ... / 20 marks

10 Complete the dialogue with the expressions in the box.

Here you are. What size are you? Not at the moment, I'm afraid. Yes, of course. It's £14.99. Can I help you?

Assistant: 1 ....

Jake: Yes, I'm looking for a black sweatshirt.

Assistant: 2 ....

Jake: I think I'm a large.

Assistant: 3 ....

Jake: I like it. How much is it?

Assistant: 4 ....

Jake: Can I try it on?

Assistant: 5 ....

Jake: Oh dear. It's a bit too big. Have you got a smaller one?

Assistant: 6 ....

Jake: Oh. OK, I'll come back later. Thanks.

Assistant: OK, bye.

1 mark per item: ... / 6 marks

Total marks: ... / 100

7A Crime scene

Vocabulary: parts of the body

1 **Label the parts of the body.**

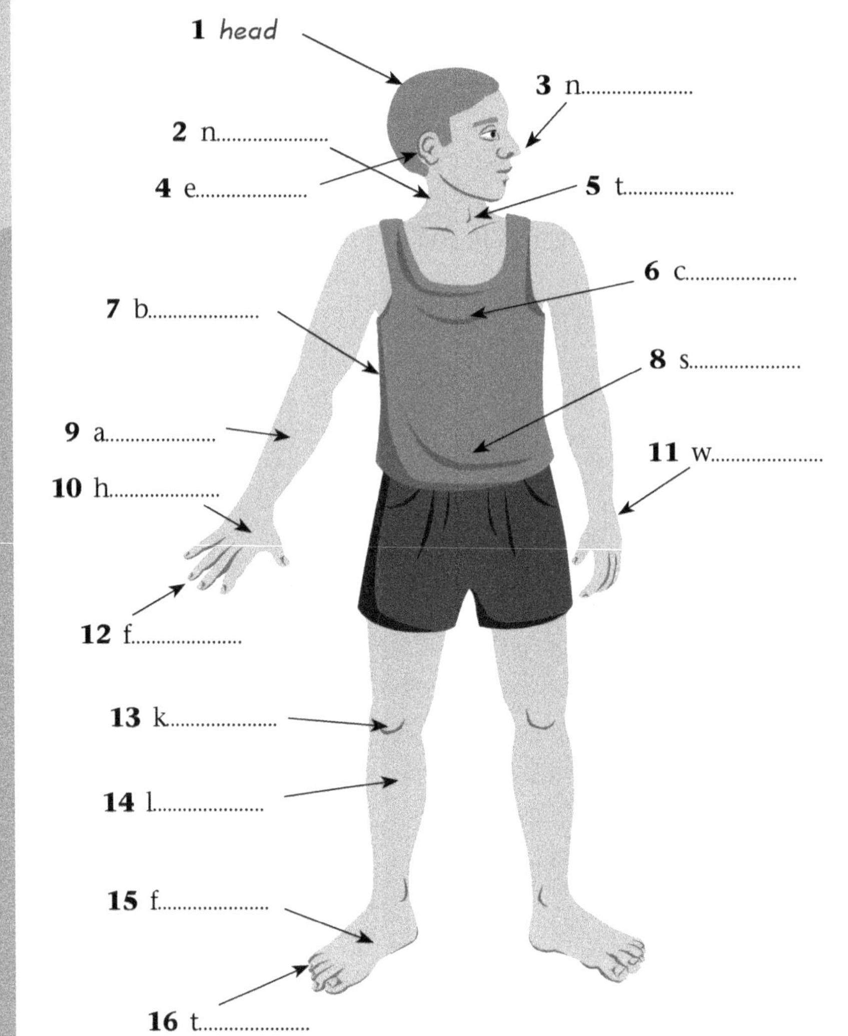

Vocabulary: crime

2 **Write the words for these definitions.**

1 A person who investigates a crime.
....

2 They wear a uniform and arrest criminals.
....

3 A crime where somebody is killed.
....

4 They saw what happened.
....

5 It is important to take some of these first!
....

6 You must find this to show what happened.
....

7 This crime takes place in a house, a bank or a shop.
....

8 A person who steals things.
....

3 **Detective Jones is talking to Police Superintendent Bates on the phone. Complete the conversation.**

Bates: Where are you Detective Jones?

Jones: Detective Johnson and I are at the [1] .... There were some [2] .... which led up the stairs, so we followed them. They led into the bathroom. The window was broken and there was some [3] .... on the floor. The thief probably cut his hand when he broke the window.

Bates: Have you got lots of evidence?

Jones: Yes. I've taken photographs and Detective Johnson has taken some [4] ....
We also found a [5] .... on the broken glass. Detective Johnson has taken some [6] ....

Bates: Good work, Jones.

Jones: And there's a [7] .... in the bedroom, but it's completely empty – the thief has taken everything!

Grammar: present perfect affirmative and negative

4 Read the conversation in Exercise 3 again. Complete the sentences with *has, hasn't, have* and *haven't*. Remember to use *'ve* and *'s* with pronouns.

Detective Jones and Johnson *have* arrived at the crime scene.

1 They .... found some footprints.
2 They .... checked for evidence.
3 They .... caught the thief.
4 Detective Johnson .... taken fingerprints.
5 He .... taken samples of blood.
6 Detective Jones .... found a safe.
7 He .... found any money in the safe.

5 Complete the table. In the fourth column write *R* (regular verb) or *I* (irregular verb).

verb	past	past participle	
break	*broke*	*broken*	*I*
....	bought	....	
....	caught	....	
check	....	....	
do	....	....	
....	found	....	
give	....	....	
have	....	....	
see	....	....	
....	spoke	....	
....	stole	....	
take	....	....	
touch	....	....	
write	....	....	

6 Complete the sentences with the affirmative or negative forms of the present perfect.

I love the film *Titanic*. I've *seen* (see) it seven times!

1 Where's my bike? Somebody .... (steal) it!
2 I'm really hungry. I .... (have) any breakfast.
3 We can't have a sandwich. Mum .... (buy) any bread.
4 'Mum, did you put my MP3 player somewhere?' 'No, I .... (touch) it.'
5 The police are still looking for evidence but they .... (find) anything.

7 Read Caroline's 'to do' list. Complete the sentences in the present perfect tense.

send an email to Josh ✓
She has sent an email to Josh

1 *do my homework ✗*
....
2 *write a letter to Aunt Mabel in New Zealand ✓*
....
3 *get photographs for my new passport ✓*
....
4 *read an English magazine ✗*
....
5 *eat some fruit ✓*
....
6 *find my favourite earrings! ✗*
....

Working with words: word pairs

8 Match (1–8) with (a–h) to make pairs of words.

1 crime	**a** camera
2 phone	**b** phone
3 film	**c** match
4 digital	**d** call
5 mobile	**e** bag
6 hockey	**f** star
7 bus	**g** scene
8 sports	**h** station

9 Complete the dialogue with pairs of words from Exercise 8.

Emily: Zac Efron is coming to a film premiere in London tomorrow! He's my favourite [1] ....

Leila: Let's go and see him! We can take photos. Have you got a [2] ....?

Emily: Yes. I have. It's an Olympus.

Leila: OK. The bus leaves the [3] .... at 9 o'clock.

Emily: Hang on! I can hear my [4] .... ringing. I've got a [5] .... from my mum. 'Hello, Mum? Yes? What time? OK. Bye!' Sorry, Leila. I can't go to London. I have to play in a [6] .... tomorrow.

7B Your health

Reading

1 Read the reports from two witnesses. Match the reports (a and b) with the witnesses (1 and 2).

1 Sam Long: shop-keeper, lives in the same street

2 Norma Carter: housewife and neighbour

a Name of witness: ....

Ms Nelson has been a customer for about three years. She has been a good neighbour; quiet but friendly. I saw Ms Nelson this morning when she came in for a newspaper. She seemed happy enough. She is usually a cheerful person. In the last few weeks, I have seen a man going to Ms Nelson's house. She doesn't often have visitors.

b Name of witness: ....

I was in my kitchen when I heard a terrible crash. It came from Fiona Nelson's house so I went to see if she was OK. The door was open. I went into the house and saw Fiona on the floor. There was blood on her face. I spoke to her but she didn't answer. I called 999 and they took her to the hospital, where she is still unconscious.

I have known Fiona a long time. She has never been married and has always led a quiet life. I've noticed that she gets up early and goes running every morning. I have often spoken to Fiona and she has always been friendly. I have never seen or heard anything that was strange – until today!

2 Who gave the following information? Write *SL* (Sam Long), *NC* (Norma Carter) or *B* (both).

Fiona Nelson is a friendly person. *B*

1 I haven't seen anything strange before. ....

2 I've seen a man at her house. ....

3 I've seen her doing sport. ....

4 Ms Nelson has bought things from my shop. ....

5 She has always been a quiet person. ....

Vocabulary: health problems

3 Write the health problems for each picture. Use the words in the box.

a cough	a broken arm	toothache	a headache	a sprained ankle
earache	sunburn	a sore throat	a cold	a fever
the flu				

1 ....

2 ....

3 ....

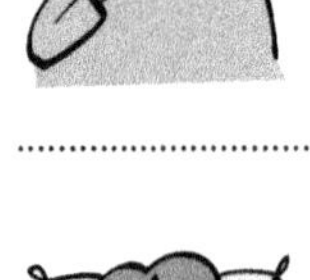

4 ....

5 ....

6 ....

7 ....

8 ....

9 ....

10 ....

11 ....

4 Complete the sentences with words from Exercise 3.

a My mum has got the flu. She's got a very high [1] .... It's more than 39°C. She can't talk or eat because she's got a [2] .... She's also got a really terrible [3] .... so we have to be very quiet. She can't sleep at night because she's got a bad [4] .... Everybody can hear her!

b My baby sister has got a [5] .... She can't wipe her nose so mum does it for her. We took her to the doctor because she was crying a lot. The doctor said she had [6] .... and gave her some medicine.

c My uncle has just come back from holiday, but he had a terrible time! On the first day he got bad [7] .... and had to spend two hours at the dentist's, which he hates. He was catching a bus back to the hotel when he fell and got a [8] .... It was difficult for him to walk after that, so he went to lie on the beach. Unfortunately, the sun was very strong that day and he got bad [9] ....!

5 Complete the sentences below with the correct expressions in the box in the present perfect.

eat all the pasta   sprain his ankle ~~not do their homework~~   buy new boots take some medicine   not see him today not start   not finish our breakfast

The teacher is angry because they *haven't done their homework.*

1 I'm sorry, you're too late for lunch! We ....
2 He can't walk home. He ....
3 I don't know where Victor is. I ....
4 You ...., haven't you? They look fantastic!
5 It's OK. You can go in, the film ....
6 I ...., but I still feel terrible!
7 We're not ready to leave. We ....

Grammar: present perfect with *ever* and *never*

6 Write *ever* or *never* in the correct position.

1 I've had bad earache.
2 Have you had a broken arm?
3 She's sprained her ankle.
4 He's had toothache.
5 Have the girls had sunburn?
6 We've smoked cigarettes.
7 Have they taken medicine?
8 My uncle has drunk alcohol.

7 Write questions and short answers using the present perfect.

you / ever / have toothache? ✓
Have you ever had toothache?
Yes, I have.

1 Leila / ever / eat meat? ✗
....
....

2 your parents / ever / have the flu? ✗
....
....

3 you and your friend / ever / have sunburn? ✓
....
....

4 your grandmother /ever / break her wrist? ✓
....
....

5 you / be a witness of / a crime? ✗
....
....

6 you / be / angry / with your parents? ✓
....
....

Listening

8 7.1 Listen to Philippa talking to a friend. Where did she go last weekend? What sport did she do?

9 Listen again and answer the questions. Choose the correct option (a, b or c).

1 Why does Philippa look terrible?
  a She's had a skiing accident.
  b She's had an operation.
  c She's been in a fight.
2 What did the two young boys do?
  a They stopped to help Philippa.
  b They caused the accident.
  c They skied with Philippa.
3 Has Karen ever broken anything?
  a Yes, she's broken her leg.
  b Yes, she's had lots of accidents.
  c No, she's never had a broken bone.
4 What has Philippa broken?
  a She's broken her legs and her tooth.
  b She's broken her tooth and her wrist.
  c She's broken her ankle and her tooth.
5 What has the dentist done?
  a He's fixed her tooth.
  b He's given her some medicine.
  c He's told her she can go to school.

7C Asking for and giving advice

Asking for and giving advice

1 Match the places (1–4) with the photos (a–d).

1 at the dentist's **2** at school
3 at home **4** at the doctor's

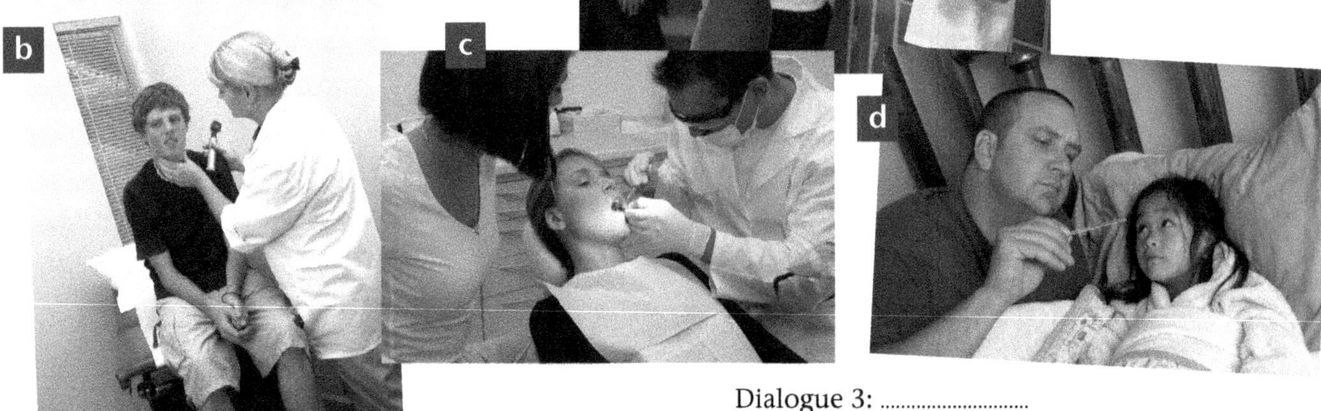

2 7.2 **Read and listen to the dialogues. Match the pictures (a–d) with the dialogues (1–3). There is one extra picture.**

Dialogue 1: ....

Doctor: Hello, Paul. What's wrong with you today?
Paul: I feel awful. I've got a sore throat and a headache.
Doctor: OK. Have you had a fever?
Paul: No, I haven't.
Doctor: Have you had earache?
Paul: No, I haven't.
Doctor: Let's have a look at your throat. Hmm … Your throat is a bit red, but it's not serious.
Paul: Right. So, what is it then, doctor?
Doctor: Well, I think you've just got a bad cold.

Dialogue 2: ....

Miss Flute: Hello, Daniel.
Daniel: Hello, Miss Flute.
Miss Flute: Oh dear, Daniel. You sound terrible. What's the matter?
Daniel: I can't come to choir, today. I've got a sore throat.
Miss Flute: What a shame! It's the concert on Saturday.
Daniel: I know!
Miss Flute: Have you taken any medicine?
Daniel: Yes, I have. I've got some throat sweets from the chemist's.

Dialogue 3: ....

Dentist: Hello, Caroline. Lie down in the chair. Now, what's wrong?
Caroline: I've got toothache. It's really bad.
Dentist: Let's see … Hmm … Does it hurt when I tap here?
Caroline: Uh-huh.
Dentist: And here?
Caroline: Uh-huh.
Dentist: Well. Everything looks OK. Have you had a cold?
Caroline: Yes, I have.
Dentist: And have you had a headache, too?
Caroline: Yes, I have. I've got one now.
Dentist: Well, your toothache is probably from your cold.

3 Put the words in the correct order to continue Dialogue 1 in Exercise 2.

Paul: I / do? / should / What
What should I do?

Doctor: should / drink / You / lots / water. / of
....

Paul: anything / I / should / else / do? / there / Is
....

Doctor: take / Yes. / can / paracetamol. / a / You
....

Paul: I / stay / in / bed? / Should
....

Doctor: you / No, / shouldn't. / few / off / But / school / for / you / should / a / days. / stay
....

Listening

4 **7.3 Listen to the whole of Dialogue 2 in Exercise 2. What advice does the teacher give Daniel? Are the sentences true or false?**

	T	F
He should buy some medicine from the chemist's.	✔	
1 He should go home to bed.		
2 He should see his doctor.		
3 He shouldn't talk.		
4 He shouldn't be in the concert.		
5 He should phone her at the school.		
6 Daniel should see the doctor before they decide about the concert.		

Pronunciation: silent letters

5 **7.4 Say the words and underline the silent letter. Then listen and check.**

1 climb
2 know
3 listen
4 answer
5 right
6 knee
7 scene
8 should
9 wrist
10 night
11 write

Writing: a personal letter

6 **Read these problems. Match the advice (1–7) with the problems (a–c). Some advice can go with more than one problem.**

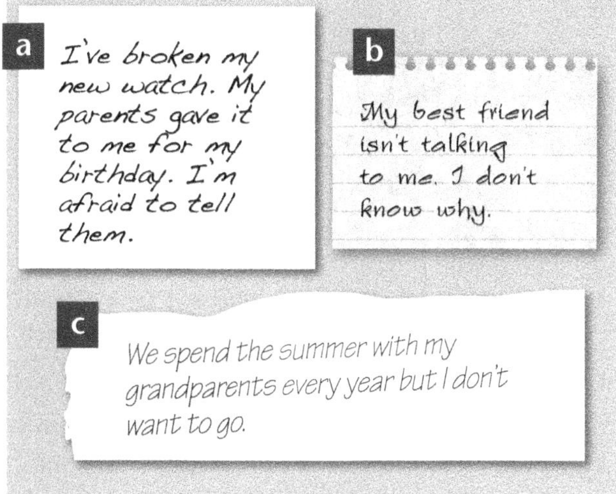

a
I've broken my new watch. My parents gave it to me for my birthday. I'm afraid to tell them.
b
My best friend isn't talking to me. I don't know why.
c
We spend the summer with my grandparents every year but I don't want to go.

I think you should talk to your parents. ....*a*....
1 You should find some new friends. ....
2 You should talk to her. Ask her what the matter is. ....
3 You should buy a new one with your own money. ....
4 You should tell your parents what's happened. ....
5 You should go and visit them for a shorter time. ....
6 Don't worry about it. ....
7 Tell your teacher about the problem. ....

7 **Choose one of the problems in Exercise 6. Imagine that a friend has written to you about this problem. Think of more advice you can give.**

You should ...
You shouldn't ...

8 **Now write a letter to your friend.**

Dear ....,
What should you do? It's not easy to give advice, but I think you ...
....
....
....
....
....
....
I hope this helps.
Best wishes,
....

9 **Check your writing.**

Check:
- spelling
- grammar
- punctuation
- word order

Look back at the last piece of writing you did. What mistakes did you make? Have you made the same mistakes again?

7D Explore more

1 Read this part of the text from Exercise 1 on page 76. Decide which option (a, b or c) is the best summary of the information.

She is usually a cheerful person. In the last few weeks, I have seen a man going to Ms Nelson's house. She doesn't often have visitors.

a Ms Nelson has a lot of visitors.
b The neighbour has seen a man at her house.
c Ms Nelson has been unhappy.

2 Now do these exercises.

1 Read the text. Decide which option (a, b or c) is the best summary of the information.

Message
For: Police Superintendent Bates
From: Detective Johnson
I've spoken to another witness at the gym. He says he has seen Fiona Nelson many times with a man. He's got blond hair and a beard. He has a tattoo on his left arm.
I think we need to talk to this man!

a The detective has spoken to a man with blond hair and a beard.
b The detective has seen Fiona Nelson at the gym.
c The detective wants to talk to a man with a tattoo.

2 Read the text. Decide which option (a, b or c) is the best summary of the information.

Daniel,
Your music teacher phoned. She hopes you are feeling better. Remember to phone her after you see the doctor. Don't forget – your appointment is at 2 o'clock.
Mum

a Daniel must see the doctor this afternoon.
b Daniel must phone his mum.
c Daniel has forgotten to phone the doctor.

3 Read this part of the text from Exercise 1 on page 76. Choose the best option (a, b or c) according to the information in the text.

I was in my kitchen when I heard a terrible crash. It came from Fiona Nelson's house so I went to see if she was OK. The door was open. I went into the house and saw Fiona on the floor. There was blood on her face. I spoke to her but she didn't answer.

a The writer describes Ms Nelson's house.
b The writer explains why she was at the house.
c The writer describes Ms Nelson's accident.

4 Read the text. Choose the best option (a, b or c) according to the information in the text.

Extreme sports can cause a lot of accidents. Every year, thousands of people have to cut short their sporting holidays because they have broken an arm or a leg. But it isn't just skiers and climbers who are injured. Footballers, rugby players and even tennis players suffer from sports injuries. Most of the time, it's just a sprained ankle or 'tennis elbow' but sometimes it can be more serious.

a The text is about adventure holidays.
b The text gives advice to sportsmen and women.
c The text describes the dangers of sport.

5 Read the text. Choose the best option (a, b or c) according to the information in the text.

Reflexology is an alternative therapy. The reflexologist pushes on parts of your feet. The idea is that parts of the foot are connected to other parts of the body and that correct massage can improve your health. The practice probably originated in China about 5,000 years ago. It is now popular all over the world but medical experts say it can be dangerous. Reflexologists do not have a lot of training and you should always see a doctor for any serious health problems.

a The text is about different health problems.
b The text is about a popular alternative medicine.
c The text is about Chinese medicine.

Word list Unit 7

advice (n) ....
ahead of (phr) ....
altitude (n) ....
ankle (n) ....
appointment (n) ....
arm (n) ....
back (n) ....
blood (n) ....
bog (n) ....
cause (v) ....
checklist (n) ....
cheerful (n) ....
chemist (n) ....
chest (n) ....
clue (n) ....
cold (adj) ....
cough (v) ....
cover (v) ....
currency (n) ....
describe (v) ....
detail (n) ....
digital (n) ....
discovery (n) ....
ear (n) ....
earache (n) ....
else (adj) ....
empty (adj) ....
evidence (n) ....
exact (adj) ....
examine (v) ....
explain (v) ....
fail an exam (phr) ....
fever (n) ....
finger (n) ....
fingerprint (n) ....
flu (n) ....
footprint (n) ....
form (n) ....
good luck (phr) ....
grip (v) ....
hairdresser (n) ....
hand (n) ....
head (n) ....
headache (n) ....
health (n) ....
hire (v) ....
improve (v) ....
injure (v) ....
investigation (n) ....
knee (n) ....
lazy (adj) ....
leg (n) ....
mark (v) ....
meat (n) ....
medicine (n) ....
mistake (n) ....
mummy (n) ....
murder (n) ....
mystery (n) ....
neck (n) ....
originally (adv) ....
originate (v) ....
owner (n) ....
personality (n) ....
poor (adj) ....
preserved (adj) ....
push (v) ....
reach (v) ....
rich (adj) ....
sacrifice (n) ....
sample (n) ....
seem (v) ....
serious (adj) ....
skilled (adj) ....
sore throat (phr) ....
spike (n) ....
sprain (v) ....
sprained (adj) ....
steal (v) ....
stomach (n) ....
suffer (v) ....
summit (n) ....
sunburn (n) ....
technique (n) ....
thief (n) ....
toe (n) ....
tooth (n) ....
toothache (n) ....
unconscious (adj) ....
valuable (adj) ....
victim (n) ....
visitor (n) ....
wet (adj) ....
yak (n) ....

U7 Reading Explorer

ahead of (phr) ....
altitude (n) ....
grip (v) ....
hire (v) ....
mark (v) ....
reach (v) ....
skilled (adj) ....
spike (n) ....
summit (n) ....
technique (n) ....
yak (n) ....

Present perfect

We use the **present perfect** to talk about actions in the recent past, but we don't know or don't mention exactly when the action happened.

*I **have found** my shoes, Mum!*	[one minute ago? one hour ago?]

We form the present perfect with ***have*** or ***has*** and the **past participle** of the main verb. With regular verbs, the past participle is the bare infinitive + ***-ed*** or ***-d***.

I've (I have) finished my homework.

He's (He has) saved the file on his computer.

Irregular verbs DON'T form the past participle by adding ***-ed***. They have a different past participle form.

Infinitive	Past	Past participle
be	was	*been*
come	came	*come*
do	did	*done*
get	got	*got*
go	went	*gone*
have	had	*had*
make	made	*made*
see	saw	*seen*

*I've **lost** Kate's Spanish book.*

*Someone **has stolen** my bike!*

We form the negative with ***haven't*** or ***hasn't*** and the past participle of the main verb.

*I **haven't** eaten anything today, so I'm really hungry!*

*He **hasn't** checked his emails.*

1 Complete the sentences with *have* or *has*. Use short forms with pronouns.

Oh no! I*'ve* accidentally locked myself out of the house!

1 You and Manuel .... collected hundreds of CDs!
2 Do you think you .... broken your arm?
3 We .... read all of these comics.
4 Paula and Jo .... packed their suitcases.
5 I .... made a list of things to do.
6 Dad .... cooked dinner for us.

2 Complete affirmative sentences in the present perfect with the verbs in brackets. Use short forms with pronouns.

Where's my mobile? I*'ve looked* (look) everywhere for it.

1 You ...... (arrive) at last!
2 We ...... (tidy) our room.
3 It ...... (stop) raining. Great!
4 My cousin ...... (watch) every episode of *Londoners*.
5 I hope that they ...... (remember) to take their keys.
6 I ...... (listen) to lots of *Coldplay* songs, but I still don't like them.

3 Complete the table of irregular verbs.

Infinitive	Past	Past participle
break	....	....
bring	....	....
buy	....	....
catch	....	....
eat	....	....
find	....	....
give	....	....
leave	....	....
lose	....	....
send	....	....
speak	....	....
steal	....	....
take	....	....
tell	....	....
write	....	....

4 Complete affirmative sentences in the present perfect with the verbs in brackets. Use short forms with pronouns.

Oh no! I*'ve lost* (lose) my mobile again!

1 Adam .... (break) his MP3 player.
2 We .... (find) a great new website about health problems.
3 Kate and Judy .... (send) us an invitation to their party.
4 You .... (eat) two double cheeseburgers! Don't you feel sick?
5 Justin's parents .... (buy) him a new computer.
6 Oh no! I .... (leave) my umbrella on the bus!

5 Complete negative sentences in the present perfect with the verbs in brackets.

We still *haven't seen* (see) the latest Johnny Depp film.

1 Dan still .... (bring) back the computer game he borrowed.

2 Don't worry – I .... (forget) we've got football practice today.
3 The police still .... (catch) the thief.
4 You still .... (read) that book I lent you.
5 Vijay .... (take) any photos with his new camera.

6 **Write sentences in the present perfect with these words.**

we / not receive / any emails from you

We haven't received any emails from you.

1 you / still not tell / me / what to do

....

2 Linda / break / her ankle

....

3 I / not speak / to anyone about the problem

....

4 Judy's friends / plan / a surprise party for her

....

5 you and Maria / write / some great songs together

....

Present perfect (questions, short answers and *ever*)

We make present perfect questions by putting ***Have/Has*** before the subject, and then the past participle of the main verb. In short answers we use ***have/has*** or ***haven't/hasn't***. We DON'T use the main verb.

We can use the word ***ever*** in present perfect questions; it always goes before the main verb.

Have you **ever** tried bungy jumping?

Has Tariq **ever** broken his arm?

7 **Write questions in the present perfect with these words.**

you / take / any medicine?

Have you taken any medicine?

1 Adam / be / to the doctor's?

....

2 the police / find / the stolen car?

....

3 we / do / well in the exam?

....

4 it / start / raining again?

....

5 you and Jessica / buy / new clothes?

....

6 I / meet / you before?

....

8 **Put these words into the correct order to make questions. Then write affirmative (✔) or negative (✘) short answers.**

been / ever / to America / you and your brother / have / ? (✘)

Have you and your brother ever been to America? No, we haven't.

1 ever / have / on a train / travelled / they / ? (✘)

....

2 Lewis / has / alcohol / drunk / ever / ? (✘)

....

3 you / watched / have / ever / a football match / ? (✔)

....

4 an exam / ever / have / I / failed / ? (✘)

....

5 ever / Joseph / a lion / seen / has / ?(✔)

....

9 **Write questions in the present perfect with *ever* and these words.**

you / have / the flu?

Have you ever had the flu?

1 Kate and Judy / smoke / cigarettes?

....

2 Frankie / climb / Mount Everest?

....

3 they / ride / a horse?

....

4 your mum / have / an accident?

....

5 you / eat / snake meat?

....

6 Ben / steal / anything?

....

Present perfect with *never*

We can form negative sentences in the present perfect with the word ***never***. It always goes before the main verb.

We've ***never*** *seen* Titanic.

My team's ***never*** *won* a match.

10 **Write negative answers to the questions in Exercise 9. Use *never*.**

(Have you ever had the flu?) *No, I've never had the flu.*

1 ....
2 ....
3 ....
4 ....
5 ....
6 ....

8A Travelling in the future

Vocabulary: transport

1 Circle the correct word for each picture.

1 a motorbike / a bike

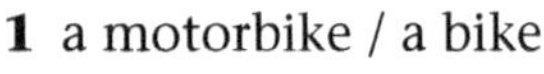

2 a spaceship / a balloon

3 a yacht / a ferry

4 a tram / a train

5 a bus / a coach

6 a boat / a yacht

2 Complete the definitions (1–6) with the words in the box.

the underground a motorbike a plane a bus a taxi a helicopter ~~a car~~

This vehicle usually carries about three passengers. *a car*

1 You catch this when it stops in the street. ....

2 It flies but it hasn't got wings. ....

3 You have to wear a helmet when you drive one of these. ....

4 If you make a phone call, one of these will come to your house. ....

5 You will probably travel on this if you go to London. ....

6 It's less expensive to fly on one of these now than it was in the past. ....

Grammar: *will*

3 Complete the sentences about holidays in the future. Use *will*/*won't* + the verb in brackets.

1 Air travel .... (not be) as cheap as it is now.

2 People .... (not have) holidays abroad.

3 There .... (be) less countryside than there is now, and more cities.

4 People .... (want to) go to the countryside for their holidays.

5 There .... (not be) any campsites.

6 People .... (stay) in enormous hotels.

7 People .... (travel) to space.

8 It .... (be) possible to have a holiday on Mars.

4 Write questions and answers about the year 2050.

everybody / shop online? (✓)

Will everybody shop online?

Yes, they will.

1 food / be more expensive?

....

Yes, ...

2 supermarkets / exist?

....

No, ...

3 people / travel by car?

....

No, ...

4 homes / be bigger or smaller?

....

I think ....

5 people / be richer or poorer?

....

I think ....

6 people / have more free time?

....

I think ....

Grammar: first conditional

5 Match the *if* phrases (1–6) with phrases (a–f).

1 If it rains,
2 If it doesn't rain,
3 If you buy your plane ticket now,
4 If you don't leave now,
5 If we look at the map,
6 If you drive too fast,

a you won't catch the bus.
b it'll be cheaper.
c the children will be carsick.
d we won't get lost.
e we'll stay in a campsite.
f we'll visit the museum.

6 Complete the sentences. Choose the correct option.

If we *don't go* / *go* / *will go* to Switzerland next winter, we'll go skiing in the Alps.

1 If you *will sit* / *don't sit* / *sit* in the sun all day, you'll get sunburnt.
2 If the children *take* / *don't take* / *won't take* toys to the beach, they'll be bored.
3 If we go to the French Riviera, we *go* / *won't go* / *will go* sailing on my uncle's yacht.
4 If you go to London, you *will need* / *need* / *won't need* a travel pass.
5 If you travel on the underground, you *will see* / *won't see* / *see* all the sights.
6 If you don't give me any stamps, I *post* / *won't post* / *don't post* your postcards!

Thursday
afternoon: Arrive in Paris — *Have dinner with Nathalie's family?*
evening: Boat trip on the river Seine
Friday
morning: Visit to the Louvre Museum — *See the Mona Lisa!*
afternoon: Climb the Eiffel Tower and visit the Tuileries Gardens — *Or the Rodin Museum? – postcard of The Kiss for Jessica*
Saturday
morning: Visit the Versailles Palace – spend the rest of the day in Versailles — *Shopping on the Champs Elysées – buy books, meet Nathalie for coffee?*
afternoon: Flight home to London at 17.30

7 Write the opposite ideas.

If we have a beach holiday, dad won't enjoy it.
If we don't have a beach holiday, dad will enjoy it.

1 If I sit in the back of the car, I'll be carsick.
....
2 If it's a nice day tomorrow, we'll go out on the boat.
....
3 If the hotel doesn't have a pool, we won't stay there.
....
4 If you miss the last bus, you'll have to take a taxi.
....

8 Daisy won't have time to do all she wants to do on her trip to Paris. Look at the itinerary with her notes and match the beginnings of the sentences (1–8) with the endings (a–h).

1 If she has dinner with Nathalie's family,
2 She won't see the *Mona Lisa*
3 If she doesn't climb the Eiffel Tower,
4 She won't spend the day in Versailles
5 She'll buy a postcard of *The Kiss* for Jessica
6 If she goes shopping on the Champs Elysées,
7 She won't meet Nathalie on Saturday
8 If she doesn't go to the Rodin Museum,

a if she goes to Versailles.
b she'll go to the Rodin Museum and buy lots of postcards.
c she won't go on the boat trip.
d she'll buy some books and meet Nathalie for coffee.
e she'll climb the Eiffel Tower and visit the Tuileries Gardens.
f if she doesn't go to the Louvre.
g if she goes shopping on the Champs Elysées.
h if she goes to the Rodin Museum.

8B Holiday plans

Reading

1 Read the text and match the photos (a–c) with the paragraphs (1–3).

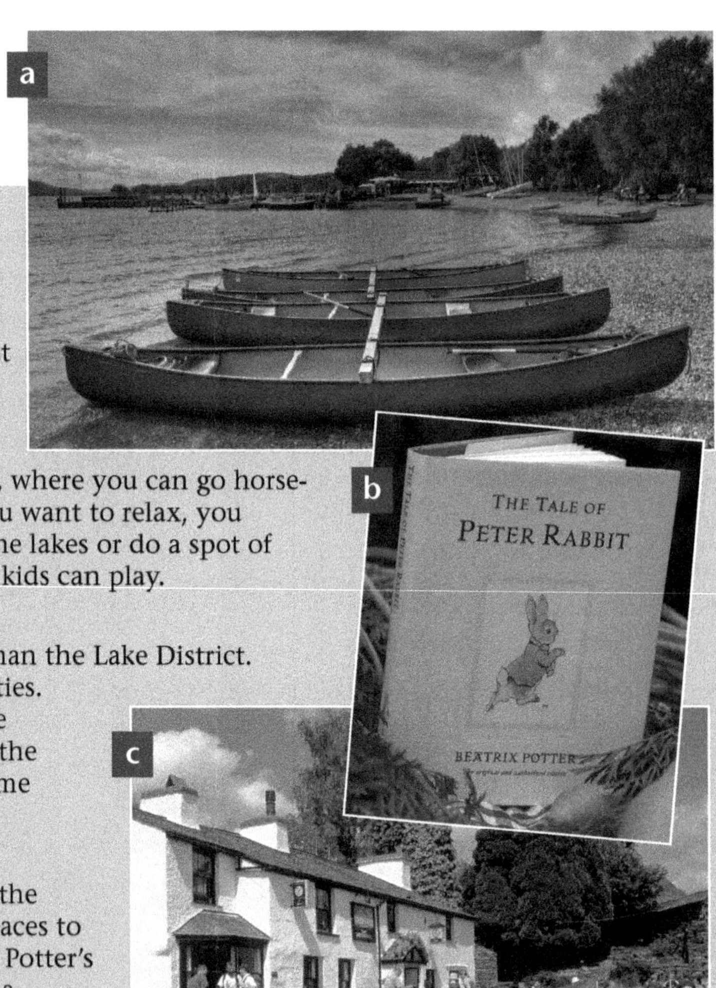

The Lake District – something for everyone!

1 ....

The Lake District is the second most popular tourist destination in the UK. As its name suggests, it's an area with many lakes but there are also hills and mountains. It's a great place for outdoor sports. You'll find activity centres in and around the lakes, where you can go horse-riding, cycling, climbing, canoeing or sailing. If you want to relax, you won't need to go far. You can sit by the shores of the lakes or do a spot of fishing. Many of the lakes have beaches where the kids can play.

2 ....

If you like walking, you won't find a better place than the Lake District. It caters for walkers and hikers of all ages and abilities. If you're a more experienced hiker, you'll enjoy the challenge of climbing Scafell Pike or Helvellyn. At the end of your walk, visit one of the local pubs for some great food and friendly service.

3 ....

If you like old buildings, you'll see lots of them in the towns and villages. There are a lot of interesting places to visit in the area. Have you ever read any of Beatrix Potter's stories? Do you know who Peter Rabbit and Jemima Puddleduck are? If you do, then a visit to Hill Top will be top of your list. Hill Top is the 17th-century farmhouse where Beatrix Potter lived. If you look carefully, you'll see a rabbit with a little blue jacket on.

2 Read the text again and answer the questions. Choose the correct option (a, b or c).

1 The Lake District:
- **a** is the most popular tourist destination in the UK.
- **b** is an area of high mountains by the sea.
- **c** has a lot of outdoor activity centres.

2 In the Lake District:
- **a** you can go swimming in the sea.
- **b** you can do water sports on the lakes.
- **c** you can't relax because it's too busy.

3 Walking in the Lake District:
- **a** is difficult, so you need a lot of experience.
- **b** is suitable for families with children.
- **c** doesn't have challenging routes for experienced hikers.

4 Other things to do in the Lake District include:
- **a** visiting old towns and villages.
- **b** doing a writing course.
- **c** studying farm animals.

5 Beatrix Potter:
- **a** was a farmer in the 17th century.
- **b** wrote books for children.
- **c** wrote stories about the hills.

Grammar: future tenses

3 Complete the sentences with *going to* or the present continuous.

1. If I go to university, I'm .... (study) chemistry.
2. My sister is .... (go) to university in September.
3. When I grow up, I'm .... (be) a fireman, like my father.
4. My grandfather .... (give) me his stamp collection one day.
5. The orchestra .... (play) in a concert on Saturday.
6. Are you .... (tell) Mum about your fight with Mark?

Reading and listening

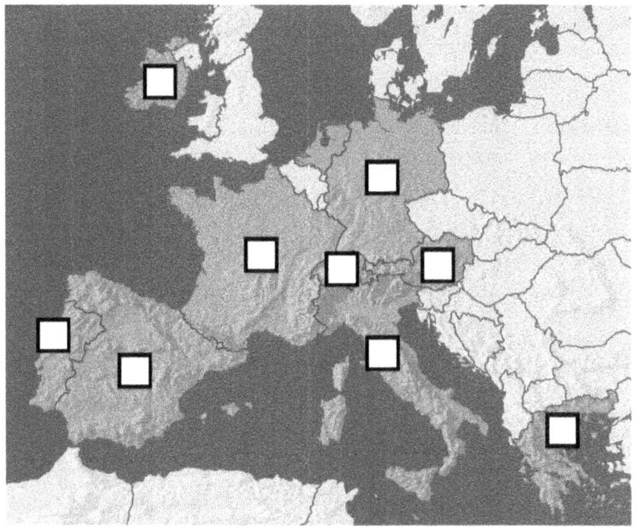

4 8.1 **Holly's family are going to travel round Europe. Read and listen to the dialogue. Write the order of the countries they are going to visit in the boxes.**

Dad: OK, everyone, let's decide where we're going to go and how we're going to get there.

Mum: Let's go to Ireland first. If we do, my Aunt Dervla will let us stay in her house on the coast.

Dad: Well, actually, I was going to suggest that we go to France first. It'll be your mum's birthday and I'm going to take her out for a romantic evening in Paris!

Holly: What about us? If you go out, who'll look after me and Jack?

Dad: Well, if we stay in a hotel for one night, there'll be a babysitting service.

Holly: Huh? No way!

Mum: If you don't like it Holly, you'll have to stay here with your grandma.

Holly: OK ... I didn't say I didn't want to come!

Dad: Good! Well next, I think we should catch the train from Paris and go to Germany. We'll go to Berlin of course, and then we'll travel south through Switzerland to Austria, then down to Italy.

Jack: What about Greece?

Dad: If we go to Greece, we won't have time to visit Spain and Portugal.

Mum: Well ... if we go to Spain last, there'll be cheap flights home from Madrid.

Holly: Great! Spanish beaches! I'm going to lie on the sand all day and get a suntan!

Jack: And I'm going to swim in the sea and catch an octopus!

Mum: And I'm going to see Aunt Dervla. If we're in Madrid, we can fly home via Dublin!

5 **Read the dialogue again and complete the sentences. Use one or two words in each space.**

If the family go to Ireland, they can stay on *the coast*.

1 In Paris, the family are going to celebrate Holly's mum's ....
2 Holly and Jack will stay in .... while their parents go out in Paris.
3 They're going to travel through Germany and Austria ....
4 After leaving Berlin, they are going to visit .... before they go to Austria.
5 Holly and Jack are going to spend time on .... in Spain.
6 If they visit Spain and Portugal, they're not going to have time to go to ....
7 Holly wants to get a(n) .... while she is in Spain.
8 At the end of the trip, they're going to fly ....

Grammar: *going to* and present continuous

6 **Holly's dad has made some final plans for their trip. Complete the text with the correct future form of the verbs.**

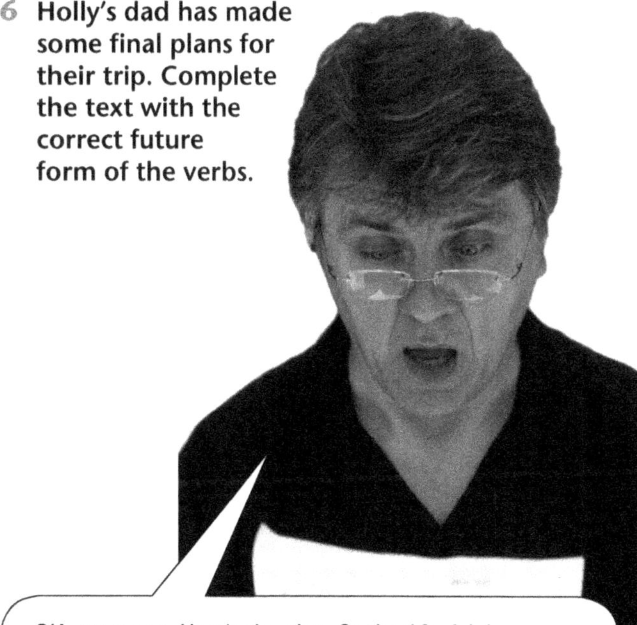

OK, everyone. Here's the plan. On the 16 of July we *'re catching* (catch) the Eurostar to Paris. We're [1] .... (visit) Paris from the 16 to the 19 and we [2] .... (stay) in a hotel. The next day, we [3] .... (take) the train to Berlin at 6 o'clock in the morning! From the 23 to the 28 of July, we [4] .... (travel) down through Germany, Austria and Switzerland. From the 29 July to the 10 August, we [5] .... (tour) round Italy.

I haven't decided exactly what the dates are after that. But don't worry, kids; we [6] .... (spend) lots of time on the beaches in Spain and Portugal.

8C Tourist information

Asking for and giving directions

1 Look at the map. Find the Tourist Information Centre and the pizzeria.

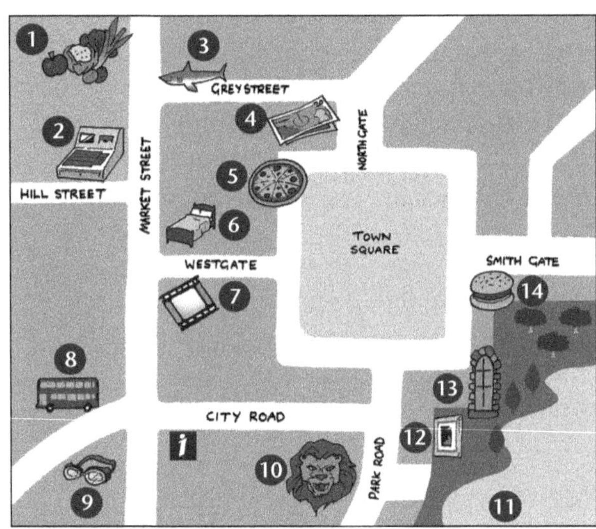

2 Now match (1–8) with (a–h) to make expressions for asking for and giving directions.

1 Is there a pizzeria
2 Yes, there is. It's
3 How do I
4 First, go along
5 Go past
6 Then turn right
7 At the end of Westgate,
8 The pizzeria's

a go into the town square.
b into Westgate.
c near here?
d about five minutes from here.
e get there?
f in the corner, on the left.
g Market Street.
h the bus station.

3 Read the dialogues at the tourist office. Follow the directions on the map and complete the information in each gap.

1

Tourist: Is there a(n) .... anywhere near here?
Assistant: Well, there's one about ten minutes from here.
Tourist: Good. How do we get there?
Assistant: It's quite easy. Just go along Market Street and it's near the end. It's on the left, opposite the aquarium.
Tourist: Thank you.
Assistant: You're welcome.

2

Tourist: Hello. Is there a(n) .... near here?
Assistant: Yes, there is. The quickest way is to go out of here and turn right. Go along City Road, and turn left at the end. Go along Park Road, across the town square and along Northgate.
Tourist: Right. That's this road here, at the opposite end of the square.
Assistant: Exactly. Then turn left into Grey Street and it's on the left.
Tourist: Great. Thanks.
Assistant: You're welcome.

4 Now complete the dialogue with words in the box.

from	opposite	welcome	past
~~can~~	end	get	along	here

Assistant: *Can* I help you?
Tourist: Is the lake near [1] ....?
Assistant: Yes, it is. It's only five minutes [2] .... here.
Tourist: Oh, good. How do we [3] .... there?
Assistant: Go out of here and walk [4] .... City Road. Turn right at the [5] .... Go [6] .... the Art Gallery. The entrance to the lake is on the left, [7] .... the zoo.
Tourist: Thanks.
Assistant: You're [8] ....

5 Two tourists are asking for directions in the street. Write the dialogue.

Tourist: Excuse. / cheap hotel / near here?
Excuse me. Is there a cheap hotel near here?

1 Man: Yes. / There's / one / ten minutes / here.

....

2 Tourist: How / get there?

....

3 Man: Go / this road / and / right / end.

....

4 Tourist: So / we / right / end?

....

5 Man: Yes. / past / museum / and / left / into / square. / hotel / in / corner.

....

6 Tourist: OK / Thank / much.

....

7 Man: You / welcome.

....

Pronunciation: syllable stress

6 8.2 **Listen to the words in the box and write them in the correct column.**

~~gallery~~	~~museum~~	fashionable	successful
anything	somebody	enormous	explorer
exciting	passenger	expensive	important
directions	beautiful		

●●●	●●●
gallery	*museum*

Writing: a postcard

7 Read Holly's postcard to Emily. Where is she? Where is she going next?

8 Tick the topics Holly talks about.

where she is
the weather
plans for tomorrow
the food
the hotel
future travel plans
the people
where she is
places she's visited / things she's done

9 Put the topics in order and complete the notes.

1 *where she is – in Vienna.*
2 ....
3 ....
4 ....
5 ....
6 ....

Hi Emily,
This is a fantastic place! We've seen lots of historic buildings and yesterday we went to the funfair. It's enormous! It's next to a beautiful, big park. The weather's been hot and sunny and I got sunburnt in the park. Tomorrow we're going to visit the art museums. Then, we're going to eat some Sacher Torte (chocolate cake) in a famous café opposite the Vienna Opera House. On Sunday, we're visiting Salzburg, where Mozart was born. Then we're taking the train through the mountains to Italy.
I'll send you a postcard from Venice.
See you at the end of August!
Love,
Holly

10 Your cousin, Sam, from Canada is staying with you on holiday. You are going to help him write his postcard. Think about your answers to the questions and write notes.

1 Where are you?
2 Where have you been?
3 What have you done?
4 What are your plans for the next few days?
5 What are your travel plans to come home?

11 Write Sam's postcard.

Dear Mum and Dad,
....
....
....
....
....
....
....
....
....
Love,
Sam

8D Explore more

Reading

1 **Read this paragraph from the text on page 86. Match the sections (1–3) with the headings (a–d). There is one extra heading.**

1 ....

The Lake District is the second most popular tourist destination in the UK. As its name suggests, it's an area with many lakes but there are also hills and mountains.

2 ....

It's a great place for outdoor sports. You'll find activity centres in and around the lakes, where you can go horse-riding, cycling, climbing, canoeing or sailing.

3 ....

If you want to relax, you won't need to go far. You can sit by the shores of the lakes or do a spot of fishing. Many of the lakes have beaches where the kids can play.

a A place to relax by the water
b A favourite holiday destination
c A summer beach holiday
d A fantastic choice of sports and activities

2 **Read the text. Match the sections (1–4) with the headings (a–e). There is one extra heading.**

1 ....

Beck's Mill is one of the best horse-riding centres in Wales. The centre is located in the heart of beautiful countryside with views of the Black Mountains. It is also a working farm.

2 ....

We offer horse-riding lessons and pony-trekking from April to October. Visitors who do not want to go out on the horses can use our fantastic indoor facilities. These include an indoor swimming pool, games room and TV room.

3 ....

Visitors can stay in small, family apartments or in shared bedrooms. The apartments have their own kitchens and bathrooms. We also serve full breakfasts and evening meals in our farmhouse kitchen.

4 ....

Families, school groups, and individuals are all welcome. Please book all holidays in advance. Our riding holidays are suitable for children over the age of ten. Children under sixteen must be part of an organised group.

a Activities and facilities
b Who can come to the centre
c Where we are
d Prices
e Accommodation and food

Listening

3 8.3 **Listen to the conversation and choose the correct option (a, b or c). You can listen to the dialogue twice.**

The vegetable market is:

a opposite Market Street on the left.
b on the left next to the aquarium.
c at the end of Market Street opposite the aquarium.

4 8.4 **Listen to the conversation and choose the correct option (a, b or c). You can listen to the conversation twice.**

The plane leaves at:

a 11.00.
b 11.30.
c 12.30.

5 8.5 **Listen to the conversation and choose the correct option (a, b or c). You can listen to the conversation twice.**

Peter:

a lives with his grandparents.
b is going to France in the summer.
c visits his grandparents three times a year.

6 8.6 **Listen to the conversation and choose the correct option (a, b or c). You can listen to the conversation twice.**

The bank is:

a next to the bookshop.
b opposite the bookshop.
c on the right.

Word list Unit 8

in advance (phr) ....
above (prep) ....
abroad (adv) ....
adventurous (adj) ....
alternative (n) ....
arrangement (n) ....
ash (n) ....
beach (n) ....
boiling (adj) ....
bubble (v) ....
bulge (n) ....
carsick (adj) ....
cater for (phr) ....
century (n) ....
challenge (n) ....
choice (n) ....
coach (n) ....
coast (n) ....
common (adj) ....
competitive (adj) ....
corner (n) ....
crack (n) ....
crater (n) ....
creativity (n) ....
designer (n) ....
destination (n) ....
directions (n) ....
discount (n) ....
edge (n) ....
elk (n) ....
entertain (v) ....
facility (n) ....
feature (n) ....
ferry (n) ....
foreign (adj) ....
funfair (n) ....
geyser (n) ....
introductory (adj) ....
itinerary (n) ....
joke (v) ....
length (n) ....
look forward (phr) ....
magma (n) ....
melted (adj) ....
moon (n) ....
mud (n) ....
octopus (n) ....
offer (v) ....
option (n) ....
own (adj) ....
package holiday (n) ....
passenger (n) ....
pool (n) ....
post box (n) ....
post office (n) ....
purpose (n) ....
rabbit (n) ....
recent (adj) ....
representation (n) ....
resort (n) ....
result (n) ....
rise (v) ....
scenery (n) ....
seasick (adj) ....
sense (n) ....
shoots into (phr v) ....
shore (n) ....
sightseeing (n) ....
space (n) ....
spaceship (n) ....
springs (n pl) ....
square (n) ....
stamp (n) ....
success (n) ....
successful (adj) ....
suitable (to/for) (phr) ....
sunbathe (v) ....
suntan (n) ....
survey (n) ....
travelcard (n) ....
underground (n) ....
weightless (adj) ....

U8 Reading Explorer

ash (n) ....
boiling (adj) ....
bubble (v) ....
bulge (n) ....
crack (n) ....
crater (n) ....
elk (n) ....
geyser (n) ....
magma (n) ....
melted (adj) ....
mud (n) ....
rise (v) ....
shoots into (phr v) ....
springs (n pl) ....

Grammar Practice Unit 8

will

We use **will** to talk about predictions about the future. We often use *will* after *I think, I hope, I'm sure*, etc.

*I think it **will** be a nice day tomorrow.*

*I'm sure people **will** live under the sea in 2110.*

Will has the same form for all subjects *(I, you, he*, etc*)*. The main verb after ***will*** is in the **bare infinitive.**

*I/We/She/etc **will** have a holiday to remember.*

The negative of ***will*** is ***won't*** *(will not)* and it is the same for all subjects.

We make questions by putting ***Will*** before the subject, and then the bare infinitive of the main verb. In short answers we use ***will*** or ***won't***. We DON'T use the main verb.

1 Complete the predictions in the affirmative (P) or negative (O) with *will* and the verbs in brackets. Use the short form with pronouns.

I'*ll be* rich and famous. (be) **P**

Most people *won't have* any problems. (have) **O**

1 Students .... online, not at school. (study) **P**
2 There .... wars and fighting. (be) **O**
3 We .... meat. (eat) **O**
4 We .... enough food for everyone. (have) **P**
5 It .... sunny and warm all the time. (be) **P**
6 People .... the flu. (get) **O**

2 Write questions about the year 2100 with *will* and these words. Then write affirmative and negative short answers, and choose which answer you believe.

there / still be / wild animals?

Will there still be wild animals?

Yes, there will. / No, there won't.

1 we / still use / computers?

....

....

2 people / live / on the Moon?

....

....

3 the air / be / clean enough to breathe?

....

....

4 there / still be / farms and farmers?

....

....

3 Write questions about the year 2100 with *will* and these words. Then write what you think.

the sea / be / cleaner or dirtier?

Will the sea be cleaner or dirtier?

I think *it will be dirtier.*

1 our lives / be / better or worse?

....

I think ....

2 transport / be / cheaper or more expensive?

....

I think ....

3 we / travel / more often or less often?

....

I think ....

4 cities / be / noisier or quieter?

....

I think ....

First conditional

We use the **first conditional** to talk about future actions or predictions based on a *condition* – that is, another future event where two things are possible.

Will it be hot tomorrow?

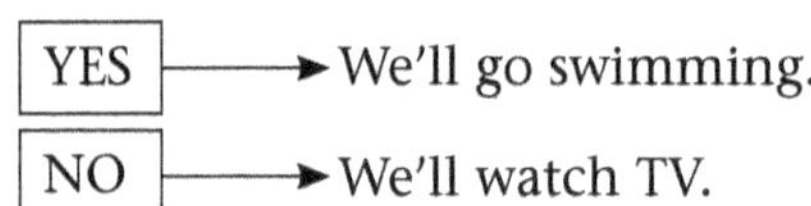

***If** it **is** hot tomorrow, we'll go swimming.*

***If** it **isn't** hot tomorrow, we'll watch TV [we won't go swimming].*

We form the first conditional with ***If*** + **present simple** for the condition, followed by ***will/won't*** for the result (the second future action or prediction). We DON'T use ***will/won't*** for the condition.

We can put the condition and the result in any order.

***If** it **rains** (NOT ~~if it will rain~~) tomorrow, I'**ll** take an umbrella.*

*Kate **won't** go to Judy's house **if** she **feels** (NOT ~~if she will feel~~) tired.*

***If** you **don't take** (NOT ~~if you won't take~~) an umbrella, you'**ll** get wet.*

4 Match (1–5) with (a–f) to make conditional sentences.

If I have enough money,	**a** it'll be cheaper.
1 I'll miss my train	**b** I'll wait at the station.
2 If I arrive early,	**c** I'll go by plane.
3 If I travel by coach,	**d** if I don't leave now.
4 I won't take a coat	**e** I'll stay at the campsite.
5 If I don't find a hotel room,	**f** if the weather is good.

5 Choose the correct words.

If it ~~rains~~ / *doesn't rain*, we'll have a picnic.

1 *I'll* / *I won't* call you if I have time.
2 If he *finds* / *doesn't find* a taxi soon, he won't catch his flight.
3 We'll have a great holiday if the weather *is* / *isn't* good.
4 If they *like* / *don't like* the place, they'll come home again.
5 I won't buy any souvenirs if *they're* / *they aren't* too expensive.

6 Choose the correct words.

If John *is* / ~~*will be*~~ late, we'll have to leave without him.

1 If you give me your address, *I send* / *I'll send* you a postcard.
2 I *don't* / *won't* hear my alarm clock if I don't go to bed soon.
3 We'll have enough money if we *spend* / *we'll spend* it carefully.
4 She'll be late if she *doesn't* / *won't* hurry.
5 If *I get* / *I'll get* bored of lying on the beach, I'll go to the museum.

7 Complete conditional sentences with the verbs in brackets. Use short forms with pronouns.

If it *isn't* (not be) cold tomorrow, we'*ll go* (go) to the beach.

1 If you .... (open) the door for me, I .... (carry) our suitcases to the car.
2 It .... (take) him days to get to Spain if he .... (go) by coach!
3 You .... (not enjoy) it if you .... (go) swimming in that cold water.
4 If Claudia .... (go) to the resort we went to, she .... (have) a great time.
5 They .... (get) lost if they .... (not take) a map.

8 Write conditional sentences with these words.

you / get / sunburnt / if / you / not put on / sun cream

You'll get sunburnt if you don't put on sun cream.

1 Karen / spend / all her money / if / she / not stop / buying souvenirs

....

2 I / not get / a suntan / if / we / not go / to the beach

....

3 if / we / hurry / we / catch / the last ferry

....

4 Kate / be / very happy / if / she and Judy / go / on holiday together

....

5 we / not fly / to the Caribbean / if / there / be / a hurricane!

....

going to and the present continuous

We use ***will*** to talk about the future when we have just decided what to do, at the time of speaking, but haven't really made any plans.

*Where can I go on holiday? I know – **I'll** go to Turkey.*

We use ***be going to*** about the future when we have already decided what to do, and have made some plans.

***I'm going to** go to Turkey this summer. I found some nice places on the Internet.*

We use the **present continuous** to talk about the future when we have made more exact plans and arrangements. When we use the present continuous in this way, we say the time or date.

***I'm** going to Turkey on 15 July. I've booked a package holiday.*

Be careful with ***be going to*** go and ***be going*** (present continuous).

I'm going to *go to Judy's house later.*	*(going to)*
I'm going *to Rome on Saturday.*	*(Present continuous)*

9 Complete the sentences with *will* or *going to* and the verbs in brackets. Use short forms for pronouns.

I'm going to meet (meet) Sonya after school, but we haven't arranged a time.

1 **A:** It's cold in here.
B: Yes, you're right. I .... (close) the window.
2 **A:** Have you got any plans for this afternoon?
B: I .... (wash) my hair.
3 **A:** Oh no! There isn't any milk!
B: Never mind. I .... (go) to the corner shop and get some.
4 **A:** Let's go to the cinema tonight.
B: Thanks, but I can't. I .... (do) my science project.

Review Units 7 and 8

1 Complete the description of a town with correct prepositions.

behind	between	in (x2)	in front of	near
next to	on	opposite	under	

1 There are some shops .... my town.
2 The shops are .... the left of the High Street.
3 There's a burger bar .... the clothes shop and the post office.
4 There's a park .... the post office.
5 There's a post box .... the post office.
6 There's a clothes shop .... the bank.
7 The supermarket is .... the park.
8 The car park is .... the supermarket.
9 There are lots of trees .... the park.
10 You can sit .... the trees when it's hot.

1 mark per item: ... / 10 marks

2 Write sentences and questions in the present perfect. Use short forms.

1 I / read / this book / six times.

....

2 you / finish / your lunch?

....

3 they / never / be / ill.

....

4 everybody / do / their homework?

....

5 you / ever / have / toothache?

....

6 somebody / steal / my bike!

....

7 you / see / my bag?

....

2 marks per item: ... / 14 marks

3 Complete the dialogues with the correct form of *will* or *going to*. Use the verb in brackets.

A: Where [1] .... on holiday this year? (go)
B: We [2] .... round France. (travel)
A: Where [3] ....? (stay)
B: We [4] .... our tent and stay in different campsites. (take)

A: In the future, I think people [5] .... to the moon for their holidays. (go)
B: No, they [6] ....!
A: Yes, they [7] ....! Richard Branson is already selling tickets online.
B: Really? I [8] .... one tomorrow! (buy)

1 mark per item: ... / 8 marks

4 Complete the text with the correct form of *going to* or present continuous. Use the verbs in brackets.

These are my plans for the summer. I haven't bought any tickets but this is what I want to do. First, I [1] .... (take) the ferry to France. Then, I [2] .... (cycle) to the south of France. My brother [3] .... (stay) there from 10 July to 9 August. I [4] .... (stay) in his hotel room and I [5] .... (relax) on the beach. Then, I [6] .... (buy) a train ticket to Spain or Italy. I [7] .... (come) back to England at the end of August because my sister [8] .... (get) married on 31 August.

1 mark per item: ... / 8 marks

5 Complete the conditional sentences with the correct form of the verbs in brackets. Use short forms.

1 If he .... (go) to France on the ferry, he .... (take) his bike.
2 If we .... (travel) round Europe, we .... (stay) in cheap hotels at night.
3 If she .... (go) on holiday to Spain, she .... (relax) on the beach.
4 If I .... (decide) to go to Italy, I .... (visit) Rome.
5 If your brother .... (get married), ... you .... (buy) him an expensive present?

2 marks per item: ... / 10 marks

6 Complete the sentences with the words in the box.

evidence	fingerprints	robbery	safe	witness

1 There was a(n) .... at the bank yesterday.

2 Two men took all the money from the ....

3 The police are looking for .... that will help them find the thief.

4 They haven't found any .... because the men were wearing gloves.

5 A(n) .... saw the men get into a blue car.

1 mark per item: ... / 5 marks

7 Read the definitions and write the words.

1 It flies in the sky without an engine. b..............................

2 I've got a blue Volkswagen Golf. c..............................

3 We sailed the Mediterranean on one. y..............................

4 The Atlantic is the largest one in the world. o..............................

5 It never rains here. d..............................

6 You can travel round London on this. The u..............................

7 It's hot and humid, with lots of trees and animals. r..............................

8 We travel on one when we go on a school trip. c..............................

9 The river meets the sea here. d..............................

10 Everest is the highest one in the world. m..............................

2 marks per item: ... / 20 marks

8 Complete the dialogue at the tourist information office with the sentences in the box.

Is it in the middle of the square? Is there a hotel near here? Thank you very much. How do we get there? Thanks. Have you got a map?

Tourist: [1] ....

Assistant: Yes. There's one in the town square.

Tourist: [2] ....

Assistant: Go down this road and turn left into the square.

Tourist: [3] ....

Assistant: No. It's in the corner on the right.

Tourist: [4] ....

Assistant: Yes. Here you are.

Tourist: [5] ....

Assistant: You're welcome.

2 marks per item: ... / 10 marks

9 Match the problems (1–3) with the advice (a–c).

1 I didn't understand anything the maths teacher said today!

2 My friend's got a terrible headache.

3 My sister studies all night and I'm worried about her.

a You should tell her to take an aspirin and go to bed early.

b You should ask her to explain the work to you.

c You should tell her not to work so hard.

2 marks per item: ... / 6 marks

10 Choose the right words to complete the dialogue.

Doctor: Good morning, Teresa. Now what's [1] *wrong / bad / cold* with you today?

Patient: Hello Doctor. I feel terrible. I've got a [2] *hurt / ache / sore* throat and a terrible head [3] *hurt / ache / sore*. I feel very hot and weak and my legs hurt.

Doctor: Mmm. Let me take your [4] *temperature / fever / hot*. Oh dear, 38.5 degrees. You've got a high [5] *fever / ache / ill*. I think you probably have the flu.

Patient: What [6] *should / have / do* I do?

Doctor: You should go straight to bed.

Patient: I'm singing in a concert on Friday. Do you think I can still go?

Doctor: No, [7] I'm *sorry / afraid / sad* not. You've got a bad case of the flu and you [8] *must / can / don't have to* rest. You [9] *shouldn't / must / have to* go out at all for the next few days. Stay at home in bed, take an aspirin every four hours and drink lots of water.

1 mark per item: ... / 9 marks

Total marks: ... / 100

Reading Explorer

Nature's fantastic performances

The sky sometimes puts on fantastic light shows. Let's look at some of these amazing performances.

Aurora Borealis lights up the night sky in Alaska

Another colourful performance from the Northern Lights.

A halo forms around the sun, usually before a storm.

What do you know?

Complete the texts. Use information from the photos to help you.

A green flash of light appears over the ocean at sunset

Rainbows

When the sun *shines* after a(n) [1] .... storm, look up into the sky. You can often see the seven colours of a *rainbow*.

***How do they happen*?**

Light from the sun *passes through raindrops*. The raindrops are like *prisms* and the light *splits* into seven different colours: red, [2] ...., ..., green, [3] ...., indigo and violet. Red is on the inside and violet is on the outside.

Auroras

Auroras happen at [4] .... Enormous *curtains* of light dance across the sky, changing shape and changing colour. They are sometimes blue, green or [5] .... They often happen in the far [6] .... and are called *Aurora Borealis*. They also happen in the far [7] .... and are called Aurora Australis.

How do they happen?

Explosions on the sun, called [8] .... winds, send hot *electric particles* into space. These particles usually hit the Earth's *magnetic field* but sometimes the particles enter the Earth's atmosphere. When these particles *collide* with gases in the atmosphere, the light show begins.

The seven colours of a rainbow appear after a rain storm in South America.

Halos

Halos are circles of light that form around the sun or the moon. They usually happen before a(n) [9] .... Never look directly at the [10] .... when you see a halo. The light can hurt your eyes.

How do they happen?

Long, thin clouds, called *cirrus clouds*, form in the sky. These clouds are made of ice crystals. The crystals *refract* the light from the sun or the moon and this forms a ring of light.

Green Flash

A green flash is a bright green light that appears when the sun sets on the horizon. The flash is very quick and they are very rare, so you don't see them often. They usually happen near the [11] ....

How do they happen?

As the sun [12] .... the sunlight passes through the *moist air* and causes a green flash of light.

Answers

Rainbows: **1** rain **2** orange yellow **3** blue
Auroras: **4** night **5** red **6** North **7** South **8** solar
Halos: **9** storm **10** sun
Green Flash: **11** ocean **12** sets

2 Reading Explorer

Dangerous jobs

Read about three scientists who have got dangerous jobs.

How dangerous do you think the jobs are? Give each job a score of 1–4.

1	= extremely dangerous
2	= very dangerous
3	= quite dangerous
4	= not very dangerous

The volcanologist

Volcanologists are scientists who study active volcanoes. They *predict* when a volcano will *erupt*. When a volcano erupts, they *give advice* to people in nearby towns and villages. They don't always work *in the field*. They sometimes work in an office as well. The volcanologist in this photo is on top of Mount Etna, which is a very active volcano in Italy. In the photo, he's collecting lava. He's wearing a helmet and a *thermal suit*. This is a dangerous job because volcanologists can *get burnt* by hot gases and *steam*. They can also be badly hurt by flying *rocks*. If a volcano suddenly erupts, the hot magma from inside the volcano can kill them. Luckily, this doesn't happen very often.

Danger score: ....

The zoologist

Wild animals can be extremely dangerous. They can attack and sometimes kill. But it's not just the animal that is dangerous. When zoologists work in the field, they often work in dangerous and difficult situations. When they want to study animals and their *behaviour*, they often put a *tracking device* onto the animals so that they can follow them. The zoologist in the photo is in the Arctic Ocean. He is sitting on the ice and trying to put a tracking device onto a *walrus*.

Danger score: ....

The tornado chaser

Severe storm researchers are meteorologists who investigate tornados and hurricanes. A tornado *chaser* follows storms and uses a *probe* to measure the *pressure* inside the tornado. They use weather forecasts and other data to predict the next tornado. As the storms form in the sky above their heads, the tornado chasers follow in cars *equipped* with *GPS*, radios, Internet connection and satellite tracking devices. They go very fast and try to arrive before the tornado. In the photo, you can see NG explorer, Tim Samaras, putting a probe *in the path of* a tornado. Sometimes, the tornado arrives just a minute or two later, and the cars and meteorologists are hit by the storm and by things flying through the air.

Danger score: ....

Which job is it?

Choose the correct job.

Who ...	volcanologist	tornado chaser	zoologist
wears a helmet?			
uses a radio?			
collects things?			
is sometimes attacked?			
drives fast?			
can get burnt?			
works in the field?			
uses a tracking device?			
can be hurt by flying things?			

Answers

volcanologist: wears a helmet, can get burnt, works in the field, can be hurt by flying things (rocks), collects things.
tornado chaser: uses a radio, drives fast, can be hurt by flying things, works in the field.
zoologist: is sometimes attacked, uses a tracking device, works in the field.

3 Reading Explorer

Madagascar!

Can you identify the animals and plants in the photos? Read the texts and complete the captions for the photos.

Animals of Madagascar

In 2005, DreamWorks made an animated film called *Madagascar*. The film follows the exciting adventures of four zoo animals that escape to the island of Madagascar. On the island they meet a lot of crazy animals, such as the aye-aye and the fossa. The aye-aye is a very strange *creature* with large eyes and ears and a long, *middle finger*. The fossa is like a dog *crossed with* a puma. It eats meat and can climb trees. But Madagascar is a real place and these amazing animals actually exist.

Geographical history

Madagascar is a large island about the size of France. It lies in the Indian Ocean, off the east coast of southern Africa. Madagascar was originally part of a super-continent called Gondwana. About 160 million years ago, Africa *broke off* from the super-continent. The island of Madagascar was formed when it broke off from the part of Gondwana which is now called India around 60 million years ago.

Unique animals and plants

When the island formed, there were no large *predators*, such as lions or big monkeys. The island was *isolated* from other continents, so old *species* survived and other, new ones *evolved*. Today, there are sixty-six *mammals* that are unique to the island, including the aye-aye, the fossa and three bird families. There are sixty types of lemur and they are all very different. The Indri lemur can sing like a *whale* and the Sifaka moves likes a ballet dancer. There are also 170 different palms, as well as six species of baobab trees which are only found on Madagascar. In total, there are more than 250,000 different species of plants, mammals, *reptiles*, and fish on the island, and 70% of these are not found anywhere else in the world. This is why Madagascar is sometimes called 'The world's eighth continent'.

1 *The .... uses its long tail to climb trees.*

3 *The .... uses its long middle finger to find insects.*

2 *The island of Madagascar is in the .... Ocean.*

Antananarivo

MADAGASCAR

Test your knowledge

Answer the questions and complete the table.

1 What was the name of the super-continent?

2 When did Madagascar break off from India?

3 Which continent is Madagascar close to?

4 Complete the table.

	plant or animal?	number of species
aye-aye	*animal*	
fossa		
lemur		
palm		
baobab		

Total number of mammals: ....

Maths challenge!

Can you do the maths? What is the total number of species unique to Madagascar?

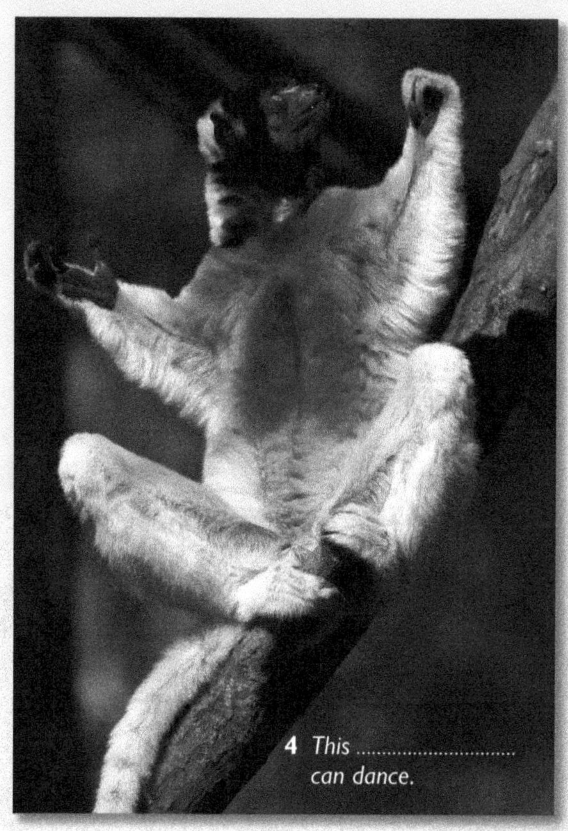

4 *This .... can dance.*

5 *This species of .... tree is unique to the island.*

Answers

1 fossa **2** Indian **3** aye-aye **4** Sifaka lemur
5 baobab

1 Gondwana
2 160 million years ago
3 Africa

	plant or animal?	number of species
aye-aye	animal	1
fossa	animal	1
lemur	animal	60
palm	plant	170
baobab	plant	6

There are 175,000 species unique to Madagascar.

4 Reading Explorer

Hair facts

Match the questions (a–f) to the texts (1–6).

a ***Why have I got hair?***

b ***How long is my hair?***

c ***How much hair have I got?***

d ***Why doesn't it hurt when I cut my hair?***

e ***Why have I got curly, brown hair?***

f ***How can I keep my hair healthy?***

1

Did you know that the hair on your head grows about five inches per year? It usually stops growing when it is three feet long. There are exceptions, of course. *The Guiness Book of Records* shows that Hoo Sateow, from Thailand, had hair which grew to 17 feet!

*inch (2.54 cm) foot (30.48 cm)

2

Hair protects your head from the weather. People whose *ancestors* lived in a hot climate had short, thick, curly hair because it protected their heads from the burning sun. People whose ancestors lived in cold climates had long, straight hair because this type of hair *traps* body *heat*. Hair also protects you if you *bang* your head.

3

To keep hair healthy, it's important to eat a healthy diet. Eat plenty of fish, cheese, eggs, brown rice and green vegetables. Your hair also produces a natural oil, called *sebum*. This is produced in the *glands*. Sebum also collects dirt, so wash your hair regularly, too.

4

Hair is made up of thousands of different *strands*. Each person has about 100,000 strands of hair. Blondes have more strands because fair hair is thinner than dark hair.

5

The only living part of your hair is the *root*, under your skin. The root produces new hair *cells* and the new cells push the old cells up out of the skin. This part of the hair is called the *shaft*. When you have your hair cut, it doesn't hurt because these cells are dead. If somebody pulls your hair, this can really hurt because they pull the hair from the root.

6

The shape of the shaft is what makes your hair straight, wavy or curly.

Straight hair has a round shaft and curly hair has a shaft which is flat. An oval shaft gives you wavy hair. Inside each shaft of hair is the natural pigment which gives your hair its natural colour.

Can you label the diagram?

1. shaft: dead part of the hair
2. gland: this is where sebum is produced
3. root: living part of the hair

Straight, curly or wavy? What's your hair type?

Hair fashion

Read about the history of hairstyles and complete the captions under the pictures (1–5). Use the expressions in the box.

1

The fashion for spiky, coloured hair ....

in ancient Rome
began in the 1970s
in the 1920s
The Ancient Greeks
The pageboy

3

.... curled their hair.

2

.... was popular in the Middle Ages.

Many of today's modern hairstyles were around centuries ago. Take the bob, for example. This short hairstyle was fashionable among women back in the 1920s. However, there was a similar style back in *the Middle Ages* when European men wore their hair down to their shoulders. This style was called the *pageboy*.

People with grey hair often colour their hair. You also see trendy teenagers today with brightly-coloured hair. This fashion started back in the 1970s when punk rockers wore their hair in amazing, *spiky* hairstyles and coloured it bright blue, red, orange and even green and purple! The first people to colour their hair were the ancient Romans, who put gold *powder* in their hair.

Curly hair was very trendy in ancient Greece. Both men and women used hot *rods* to make their hair curly. These were probably the first *curling irons*. In the 1980s, women wanted lots of long, curly hair. Nowadays, the fashion is for long, straight hair.

4

Golden hair was trendy ....

5

The bob became fashionable ....

Answers
1b **2**a **3**f **4**c **5**d **6**e
1 began in the 1970s **2** the pageboy
3 the Ancient Greeks **4** in ancient Rome
5 in the 1920s.

5 Reading Explorer

Deadly creatures

Read about some of the world's deadliest creatures. Complete the texts (1–7) with the names of the animals in the box.

blue-ringed octopus	box jellyfish
black widow spider	Gila monster
eyelash viper snake	stingray
rainforest frog	

The poison that some animals make is called *venom*. Venom helps these animals to survive in nature. Most venom is deadly, which means that these animals can kill.

Poisonous animals use their venom to kill other creatures for food or to fight off their attackers.

Some venom can kill people, too. So, is it safe to leave the house?

1

The .... is an insect which is famous for its poison. In fact, some experts say that its poison is many times more powerful than a *rattlesnake*'s. It catches its *prey* in its *web*, and then bites the animal with its poisonous *fangs*. Sometimes the body of the insect it catches is too hard to eat, but the venom makes it softer.

2

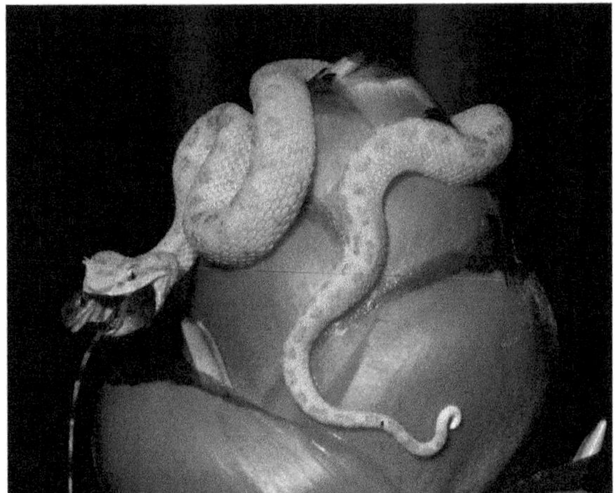

There are many venomous snakes but the .... is the most poisonous. It has poisonous fangs inside its mouth. This snake eats birds, rats, frogs and other small animals. When it finds its prey, it moves fast. Its fangs come out and it bites the animal. The animal's heart stops and then the snake can eat it.

3

One of the world's deadliest creatures lives deep under the sea. The .... has a square body and long poisonous *tentacles*. Some of these tentacles can be more than 14 feet long. If a fish gets too close, it touches the tentacles and the poison kills it.

4

The .... is the second deadliest creature on Earth. It also lives in the ocean. This animal kills crabs, but scientists do not really understand how. It has tentacles but some experts believe that it *spits* its poison into the sea. The crab dies when the venom enters the crab's body.

5

Another deadly sea creature lives down at the bottom of the ocean. The .... has *spines* full of poison and hides on the sea bed. It is the same colour as the sand and it waits until its prey comes past. The passing sea creature doesn't know it's there until the spine quickly shoots venom into its body. But, by then, it's too late!

6

These animals are a lot easier to see. They are bright green, yellow, red or green and their amazing bright colours *warn* other animals that they are poisonous. The .... has poison in its skin. South American Indians put the poison on their darts when they go hunting.

7

So, is it safe enough to go out and explore nature?

Don't be too frightened. Most poisonous animals only attack when they feel *threatened*, and some of them can actually help people who are ill. For example, the venom from frogs is a stronger *painkiller* than aspirin, and doctors are using poison from a(n) .... lizard to treat people with *diabetes*.

Write the answers to the quiz.

Quiz: Deadly creatures

1 Which animal is the deadliest – a rattlesnake or a black widow spider?

2 Which poisonous animal is the most colourful?

3 Which creature is the most difficult to see?

4 Which two animals have got venom that can help people?

5 Which people use poison when they go hunting?

6 Which is the most poisonous part of an eyelash viper?

7 Which sea creature has the longest tentacles?

Answers

1 black widow spider **2** eyelash viper snake
3 box jellyfish **4** blue-ringed octopus **5** stingray
6 rainforest frog **7** Gila monster

Quiz

1 black widow spider **2** rainforest frog **3** stingray
4 rainforest frog, Gila monster lizard
5 South American Indians **6** fangs **7** box jellyfish

Nature's sweet shop

Sugar

Have you got *a sweet tooth*?

Everybody loves something sweet. Who doesn't enjoy cakes, chocolate or biscuits?

But did you know that there is sugar in a lot of the food we eat these days? Sugar is added to orange juice, breakfast cereals and fizzy drinks. No surprise there. But what about cans of tomatoes, cans of beans or cold meat? Do you think there's any sugar in them? Well, the surprising answer is 'yes'. And we can add a lot of other *processed food* to the list, such as yoghurt, pizza and bread.

So where does sugar come from? Sugar comes from a plant called *sugarcane*. Sugarcane isn't easy to grow. It needs lots of water, good *soil* and bright sunshine. The sugarcane grows taller and taller and the juice inside the *stalk* grows sweeter and sweeter. It takes between eight months and twenty-two months for the sugarcane to be ready for *harvest*.

At that point, workers can cut down the sugarcane stalks. They use machines to *crush* the stalks and *squeeze out* all the sweet juice. Next, the juice boils in large pots where it forms a *sticky mass* of small *grains* and syrup. More machines separate the grains from the syrup to produce sugar grains.

Read the text about sugar. Are the sentences true or false?

	T	F
1 There is some sugar in breakfast cereal.	☐	☐
2 There is no sugar in meat.	☐	☐
3 Sugarcane must have lots of sunshine to grow.	☐	☐
4 Sugarcane grows fast.	☐	☐
5 The tallest stalks have the sweetest juice.	☐	☐
6 There are grains of sugar inside the stalks.	☐	☐
7 Machines crush the stalks to make a juice.	☐	☐
8 When the juice boils it forms a syrup.	☐	☐
9 There aren't any grains of sugar in the syrup.	☐	☐

Three boys with stalks of sugarcane in the Sierra Maestra region of Cuba.

Chocolate

Dark chocolate, milk chocolate, white chocolate, chocolate eggs, chocolate cake, or chocolate sauce: is there anything sweeter, and more delicious, than chocolate?

That's why it's difficult to believe that the beautiful chocolates in the photo began as ugly, white beans.

So where exactly does chocolate come from?

Chocolate comes from cacao trees. Cacao trees grow in parts of the world which have a tropical climate, such as South America or South East Asia. The trees have large, brightly-coloured fruit, or *pods*, which come in different *shades* of yellow, orange, red, green or purple. Each pod is full of white beans. To get the beans, workers must cut the pods off the trees and *crack them open*.

The workers put the beans in very large bins and leave them for some days. The beans start to change inside. They get darker and develop their chocolaty taste. Then the workers *roast* and *grind* the beans to make a brown powder.

In the past, people mixed some of the powder with water and made a drink. It didn't have any sugar in it and it tasted *bitter*. Today, chocolatiers (chocolate makers) add sugar and milk to the cacao powder to make it taste sweet.

From this,

... to this.

Read the text about chocolate. Find the answers to these questions.

1 What colour is chocolate?
2 What colour are cacao beans?
3 What colour is the fruit from the cacao tree?
4 What colour is cacao *powder*?

Complete the health tip below.

A worker cuts down pods from a cacao tree.

Health tip!

Too much sugar can be bad for you. Everybody knows it's bad for your teeth, but it can also cause an illness called diabetes that can affect children and young people. This doesn't mean you mustn't eat any sugar at all. Just try to follow these simple rules:

- Don't eat too much [1] p.............................. food.
- Don't eat too many [2] c.............................. and biscuits.
- Eat some fresh [3] v.............................. and [4] f.............................. everyday.
- Don't have a lot of sugary [5] d..............................
- Drink lots of [6] w..............................

Answers

1 T **2** F **3** T **4** F **5** T **6** F **7** T **8** T **9** F

1 brown **2** white **3** yellow, orange, red, green or purple **4** brown

1 processed **2** cakes **3** vegetables **4** fruit **5** drinks **6** water

7 Reading Explorer

Climbing the Himalayas

Read the text and match the paragraphs (1–4) with the headings (a–d).

a The Sherpas' story **b** A dangerous job **c** Sherpa school **d** Kili's ambition

1 ....

Kili Sherpa always knew what he wanted to be when he grew up. He wanted to be a mountain climber and climb the mountains around his village, in Nepal. These mountains are the Himalayas – the highest mountains in the world.

Some of Kili's family have climbed the Himalayas. They have worked as guides and helpers on many climbing expeditions. When he was a boy, Kili loved listening to their stories and he practised hard to be a climber. He grew up to become a *skilled* climber and guide, and *reached* the *summit* of Mount Everest in 2000.

2 ....

Kili's people are called Sherpas. They originally lived in Tibet but they moved to Nepal in the early 1500s. They built villages in the mountains and grew vegetables and kept *yaks*. They spoke their own language and kept their Tibetan traditions. They believed that the mountains were the homes of their *gods*. They didn't climb the mountains until about 400 years later.

In the early 1900s, a British explorer, Alexander Hellas, *hired* Sherpas to carry equipment up the mountains. Hellas was amazed by the Sherpas. They were strong, brave and worked extremely hard. After that, the Sherpas became helpers on nearly every climbing expedition and, in May 1963, a Sherpa named Tenzing Norgay was the first person to be photographed at the top of Mount Everest. In fact, Sherpa Tenzing and Edmund Hillary, from New Zealand, were the first climbers to reach the summit of Everest.

3 ....

Today, there are many expeditions to Everest. The Sherpas look after equipment, put up campsites and cook. Their job is also dangerous. They *mark* the routes up the mountain *ahead* of the climbers. More than 150 people have died on Everest. Climbers have died in storms and *avalanches*. They have also got sick because the *altitude* is too high for them. In the past, young Sherpas with no training worked on the expeditions. Kili Sherpa thought it was too dangerous for them, and that they should learn some basic techniques.

4 ....

In 1996, Kili opened The Solu-Khumba Sherpa Climbing School. Children and adults go there to learn the basics of climbing and the lessons are free. Students spend many days training and climbing with Kili. Then they begin doing simple jobs on short expeditions. It can take many years before they go on important climbs, but some of Kili's earliest students have even worked on Everest expeditions!

Students at the Solu-Khumba Climbing School learn to climb large rocks before they climb the Himalayas.

Basic Climbing Skills

Have you ever wanted to go mountain climbing?

Before you go, you should go to a climbing school and learn some basic skills.

First, you will need to know your equipment. A climber needs ropes, a *harness*, climbing boots with crampons and a helmet. Crampons are metal *spikes* on the boots, which *grip* the ice. A harness goes around your waist and between your legs. You attach your ropes and crampons to it. A helmet, of course, protects your head.

You will also need to learn three important techniques:

belaying holding ropes for another climber.

jumaring using special tools to grip the ropes and climb up.

rappelling sliding down a rope.

When you are at high altitudes, these skills must be automatic.

Test your climbing knowledge.

1 Where did the Sherpa people come from?

2 When did the Sherpas start climbing mountains?

3 Who were the first people to reach the top of Mount Everest?

4 How many people have died on Everest?

5 Why do some climbers get sick?

6 When did Kili Sherpa open his climbing school?

7 Label the drawing.

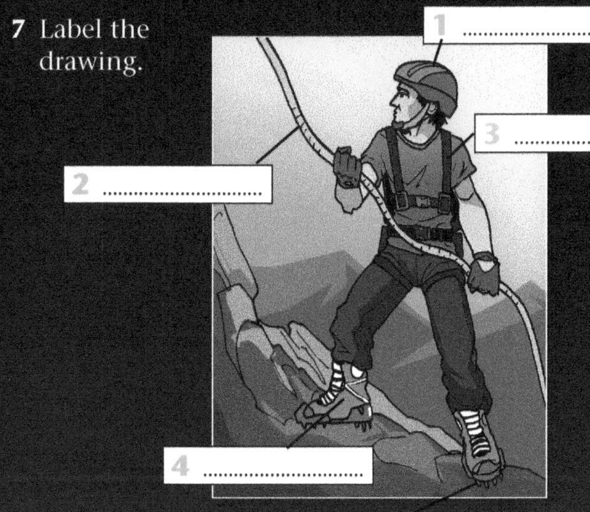

8 What is Kili doing in this photo? Complete the caption.

In this photo, Kili Sherpa .... for one of his students.

Sherpa Tenzing at the summit of Mount Everest.

Answers

1d **2**a **3**b **4**c

1 Tibet **2** the early 1900s

3 Tenzing Norgay and Edmund Hillary

4 150 **5** because of the high altitude **6** 1996

7 1 a helmet 2 a rope 3 harness 4 boots 5 crampons

8 is belaying

Yellowstone

If you like fantastic scenery and wild animals, you will love Yellowstone!

Yellowstone National Park in the USA became the world's first national park in 1872.

It is a very special place. The park formed thousands of years ago, as the result of volcanic activity. There are spectacular, high cliffs of volcanic rock with enormous waterfalls and many lakes. The park's largest lake, Yellowstone Lake, is actually a volcanic crater.

There is evidence of volcanoes everywhere in Yellowstone. There are many *hot springs*, and some rivers are full of *boiling* water. Pools *bubble* with hot water and *mud*. There are more than 300 geysers – more than anywhere else on Earth. The most famous geyser is called Old Faithful. Every 90 minutes a day, a tower of water and steam *shoots out* of the earth. It is incredibly noisy and smells like bad eggs. The smell comes from a mixture of gases and water. Then the noise and water suddenly stop, and it is quiet again.

The park's forests are home to some amazing wildlife, including wild bears, bison and *elk*. One of the park's most interesting places is the petrified forest. When the park formed, heat and minerals from *melted* rocks turned the trees to stone. The forest is not easy to find and most visitors have never seen it.

Complete the tourist information below.

Tourist Advice

Getting there

You can travel by (1) .... to three main airports. There are no buses from two of the airports, so you will have to rent a(n) (2) .... and drive to Yellowstone.

Where to stay

If you stay in the park, you will have lots of accommodation to choose from, including hotels and cabins. Hikers can take a (3) .... and stay at different campsites inside the park.

What to see

(4) ....: the most famous geyser in the park.

(5) ....: a forest turned to stone (if you can find it!).

(6) ....: a huge crater, which is full of water.

Wildlife: (7) .... and elk.

Old Faithful is the most famous geyser in Yellowstone Park.

Match the questions (a–c) with the paragraphs (1–3). Then label the diagram.

a What will happen if the volcano erupts?

b How will people know if the volcano is going to erupt?

c Where does all the hot water in Yellowstone come from?

1 ....

The answer lies deep underground. *Melted* rock called magma heats the rock under the earth's surface. This hot rock heats underground springs and the hot water *rises* to the surface through *cracks* in the rocks. Geysers have hot steam as well as water, and this causes them to erupt.

2 ....

The magma under Yellowstone Park forms part of one of the largest volcanoes in the world. It has erupted many times. The most recent eruption was 640,000 years ago. If it erupts again, people will hear the noise all around the world. Hot *ash* will fill the sky and people won't see the sun for many months. If this happens, temperatures will fall and some plants and animals will die.

3 ....

Nowadays, scientists can predict volcanic eruptions. Before a volcano erupts, the magma will start to rise and the ground will *bulge*. Scientists have put special equipment around the park which shows that the ground is not bulging. There will also be lots of strong earthquakes first. This is not happening at the moment.

underground spring
magma
geyser
hot rock

1 ....
2 ....
3 ....
4 ....

A hot spring in Yellowstone National Park.

Answers

1 plane **2** car **3** tent **4** Old Faithful **5** The petrified forest **6** Yellowstone Lake **7** wild bears and bison.
1 c **2** a **3** b
1 geyser **2** underground spring **3** hot rock **4** magma